RAMTHA

RAMTHA

ISBN 1-57873-017-1
Library of Congress Card Number: 85-61768

Other Titles by JZK Publishing

The Mystery of Love
The Plane of Bliss
A Beginner's Guide To Creating Reality
The Children's View of Destiny and Purpose

JZK Publishing
P.O. Box 1210
Yelm, Washington 98597 USA
360.458.5201
800.347.0439
www.ramtha.com / info@ramtha.com

CONTENTS

To God
who lives
within you

CHAPTER 1

Introduction

There is no other redemption for mankind than to realize
their divinity. You are the seeds of this realization.

I am Ramtha, a sovereign entity, who lived a long time ago upon this plane called Earth, or Terra. In that life I did not die; I ascended, for I learned to harness the power of my mind and to take my body with me into an unseen dimension of life. In doing so, I realized an existence of unlimited freedom, unlimited joy, unlimited life. Others who lived here after me have also ascended.

I am now part of an unseen brotherhood who loves mankind greatly. We are your brothers who hear your prayers and your meditations and observe your movements to and fro. We are those who lived here as man and experienced the despair, the sorrow, and the joy that all of you have known. Yet we learned to master and transcend the limitations of the human experience to realize a grander state of being.

I have come to tell you that you are very important and precious to us because the life that flows through you and the thought that is coming to every one of you — however you entertain it — are the intelligence and life force that you have termed God. It is this essence that connects all of us, not only to those upon your plane but to those in untold universes which you have not yet the eyes to see.

I am here to remind you of a heritage which most of you forgot long, long ago. I have come to give you a loftier perspective from which you may reason and understand that you are indeed divine and immortal entities who have always been loved and supported by the essence called God. I am here to help you realize that only you, through your sublime intelligence, have created every reality in your life and, with that same power, you have the option to create and experience any reality you desire.

Many others have come to you throughout your history, and they have tried many different avenues to remind you of your greatness, your power, and the foreverness of your lives. We have been king, conqueror, slave, hero, crucified Christ, teacher, guide, friend, philosopher — anything that would permit knowledge to occur. And at times we have intervened in your affairs to keep you from annihilating yourselves so that life here would continue to provide a playground for your experiences and your evolution into joy. But one by one you persecuted those who reached out to help you. Those you didn't persecute, you made statues of and you twisted and perverted their words for your own designs. Instead of applying their teachings, many of you have ended up worshiping the teachers.

To prevent your worshiping me, I have not come to you in my own embodiment. Instead I have chosen to speak to you through an entity who was my beloved daughter when I lived upon this plane. My daughter, who graciously allows me to use her embodiment, is what is termed a pure channel for the essence that I am. When I speak to you, she is no longer within her body, for her soul and Spirit have left it completely.

I have brought with me the winds of change upon your plane. I and those who stand with me are preparing mankind for a grand event that has already been set into motion. We are going to unite all the people of this plane by allowing man to witness something great and brilliant, which will cause him to open up and allow knowledge and love to flow forth.

Why is this being done? Because you are loved greater than you have ever considered love to be and because it is time for man to live a grander understanding than that which has plagued him into dark ages, taken away his freedom, divided peoples, and caused hatred between lovers and war amongst nations. It is time for that to be finished. It is time for man to realize his divinity and immortality of being and cease groveling for survival upon this plane.

There is coming a day very soon when great knowledge will be brought to this plane by wonderful entities who are your beloved brothers. In that time, scientific developments will bloom here greater than they ever have. What is coming forth is called the Age of God. This age will come about through a deliberate change in time and the values of time. In the years to come, disease, suffering, hatred, and war will no longer be upon this plane. No longer will there be the aging and death of the body, but continuous life. It is through knowledge, understanding, and profound love that these things will come forth in the life of each entity.

There is no other redemption for mankind than to realize their divinity. You are the seeds of this understanding. As each of you realize your own worth and value and the foreverness of your life, you will add, one by one, to the consciousness of unlimited thinking, unlimited freedom, and unlimited love. Whatever you think, whatever you come to realize, lifts and expands consciousness everywhere. And when you live what you have come to understand, wholly for the good of your own purposeful life, you allow others to see in you a greater thought process, a grander understanding, a more purposeful existence than what they see all around them.

These times are the greatest of all times in your recorded history. Though they are difficult and challenging times, you chose to live here during this time for the purpose of the fulfillment that it would bring you. All of you have been promised for e'er so long that you would see God in your lifetime, yet lifetime after lifetime you never allowed yourselves to see it. In this lifetime, most of you will indeed. You will see a magnificent kingdom emerge here, and civilizations will come forth that you had not even the slightest notion existed. And a new wind will blow. And love, peace, and joy in being will grace this blessed place, the emerald of your universe and the home of God.

Contemplate what is spoken. Allow these words into your

being. When you do, thought by thought, feeling by feeling, moment by moment, you will come back into the understanding of your greatness, your power, and your glory.

**

CHAPTER 2

I Am Ramtha

*I am Ram the Conqueror, now Ram the God. I was a
barbarian who became God through the simplest
and yet the most profound of things. What I teach
you is what I learned.*

I am Ramtha, the Ram. In the ancient language of my
times it means "the God." I am the great Ram of the Hindu
people, for I was the first man born of the womb of woman and
the loins of man who ever ascended from this plane. I learned
how to ascend not through the teachings of any man but through
an innate understanding of the God that lives in everything. I
was also a man who hated and despised, who slew and conquered
and ruled right into my enlightenment.

I was the first conqueror this plane knew. I began a march
that lasted sixty-three years, and I conquered three-quarters of
the known world. But my greatest conquest was of myself, coming
to terms with my own existence. When I learned to love myself
and embrace the whole of life, I ascended with the wind into
forever.

I ascended in front of my people on the northeast side of
the mount called Indus. My people, who numbered more than
two million, were a mixture of Lemurians, the people from Ionia
— later to be termed Macedonia — and the tribespeople escaping
from Atlatia, the land you call Atlantis. It is my people's lineage
that now makes up the populace of India, Tibet, Nepal, and
Southern Mongolia.

I lived but one lifetime upon this plane, what is called in
your understanding of time, 35,000 years ago. I was born in

ignorance and desperation to an unfortunate people, pilgrims from the land called Lemuria, living in the slums of Onai, the greatest port city of Atlatia in its southern sphere. I came to Atlatia during what is called the last hundred years, before the continent broke up and great waters covered its land.

At that time Atlatia was a civilization of people with great intellect, whose endowment for scientific understanding was superb. Their science was even greater than what you have at this time in your scientific community, for the Atlatians had begun to understand and use the principles of light. They knew how to transform light into pure energy through what you term lasers. They even had aeroships that traveled on light, a science provided to them through an intercommunication with entities from other star systems. Though their ships were very primitive, they were nonetheless mobile and airborne. Because of the Atlatians' great involvement with technology, they worshiped the intellect. Thus intellectual science became the religion of the Atlatians.

The Lemurians were quite different from the Atlatians. Their social system was built upon communication through thought. They had not the advancement of technology, only a great spiritual understanding, for my forefathers were great in their knowingness of unseen values. They worshiped and revered that which was beyond the moon, beyond the stars. They loved an essence that could not be identified. It was a power they called the Unknown God. Because the Lemurians worshiped only this God, the Atlatians despised them, for they despised anything that was not progressive.

In the days of the Ram when I was a little boy, life was destitute and very arduous. At that particular point in time Atlatia had already lost its technology, for its scientific centers in the north had been destroyed long ago. In their experiments with traveling on light, the Atlatians had pierced the cloud cover that completely surrounded your planet, much as it surrounds Venus today. When they pierced the stratosphere, great waters fell and a freeze occurred, which put most of Lemuria and the northern parts of Atlatia under great oceans; thus the people from Lemuria and the north of Atlatia fled to the southern regions of Atlatia.

Once technology was lost in the north, life gradually became primitive in the south. During the hundred years before all of Atlatia was submerged, the southernmost region was a primitive Atlatia that had degenerated into the rule of tyrants. The tyrants governed the people not through a republic but through irrefutable law. In the government of irrefutable law, the Lemurians were considered the dung of the earth, less than a dog in the street.

Contemplate for a moment being spat upon, urinated upon, and allowed to wash it away only with your tears. Contemplate knowing that the dogs in the streets have greater nourishment than you who hunger for anything to kill the agony in your belly.

In the streets of Onai, it was common to see the brutalization of children and the beating and rape of women. It was common to see Atlatians pass a starving Lemurian on the road and hold their noses with kerchiefs of fine linen dipped in jasmine and rose water, for we were considered stinking, wretched things. We were the no-things, the soulless, mindless wastes of intellect because we were without the scientific understanding of such things as gases and light. Because we did not possess an intellectual bent, as it were, we were turned into slaves to work the fields.

That was when I was born upon this plane. That was my time. What sort of dream was I in? The advent of man into the arrogance and stupidity of intellect.

I did not blame my mother that I did not know who my father was. I did not blame my brother that our fathers were not the same, nor did I blame my mother for our absolute poverty. As a little boy I watched as my mother was taken into the streets and had her sweetness taken from her. After my mother was taken, I watched a child grow inside her belly and I knew whose it was. And I watched my mother weep, for would there be another child in the streets to suffer as we had suffered in this Promised Land?

Because my mother was too weak to bear the child alone, I helped her give birth to my little sister. I scrounged in the streets for food, killed dogs and wildfowl, and stole grain from proprietors late in the evening, for I was very deft on my feet. I fed my mother, who in turn suckled my little sister.

I did not blame my little sister for the death of my beloved mother, for the little girl suckled away all of my mother's strength. My sister became diarrhetic and could not hold what was going into her body, and so she too lost all the life in her body.

I laid my mother and sister together and went to gather timbers. I put the timbers on top of them and stole away into the night to gather fire. I said a prayer to my mother and my sister, whom I loved greatly. Then I lit the timbers swiftly so that the stench from their bodies would not disturb the Atlatians for, if it did, the Atlatians would fling their bodies into the desert where the hyenas would prey upon them and tear them apart.

As I watched my mother and sister burn, my hatred for the Atlatians increased within my being to where it became like venom from a great viper. And I was only a little boy.

As the stench and smoke from the fire spread throughout the valley, I thought about the Unknown God of my people. I could not understand the injustice of this great God or why he would create the monsters that hated my people so. What did my mother and little sister ever do to deserve the wretched deaths they experienced?

I did not blame the Unknown God for his inability to love me. I did not blame him for not loving my people. I did not blame him for the death of my mother and my little sister. I did not blame him; I hated him.

I had no one left, for my brother was kidnapped by a satrap and taken into subserviency into the land that would later be called Persia. There he was abused for the pleasure of the satrap and his need for what is called loin gratification.

I was a lad of fourteen with no meat upon my bones and a great bitterness inside me. So I decided to do battle with the Unknown God of my forefathers, the only thing I felt worthy of dying by. I was determined to die, but as an honorable man. And I felt that dying at the hands of man was a dishonorable way to perish.

I saw a great mountain, a very mysterious place that

loomed on the distant horizon. I thought that if there were a God, he would live there, above us all, just as those who governed our land lived above us. If I could climb there, I thought, I would get in touch with the Unknown God and proclaim my hatred for him at his unfairness to humanity.

I left my hovel and journeyed for many days to reach this great mountain, devouring locusts and ants and roots along the way. When I reached the mount, I climbed into the clouds, which now veiled its whitened peak, in order to do battle with the Unknown God. I called out to him, "I am a man. Why have I not the dignity of one?" And I demanded that he show me his face, but he ignored me.

I fell upon my haunches and wept heartily, until the whiteness iced itself from my tears. When I looked up, I beheld what seemed to be a wondrous woman holding a great sword before me. She spoke to me saying, "O Ram, O Ram, you who are broken in Spirit, your prayers have been heard. Take this sword and conquer yourself." And in but a blink of my eye she was gone.

Conquer myself? I could not turn the blade around and hack off my own head; my arms would not reach the hilt of the sword. Yet I found honor in this great sword. No longer did I shiver against the great cold but found warmth instead. And when I looked again where my tears had fallen, there grew a flower of such sweet aroma and color that I knew the flower was of hope.

I came down from the mountain with the great sword in my hand, a day which was recorded in the history of the Hindu people as the Terrible Day of the Ram. A boy had gone to that mountain, but a man returned. No longer frail or weak of bodily movement, I was a Ram in every sense of the word. I was a young man with a terrible light about me and a sword that was larger than I was. Sometimes I think I was very slow to understand in that existence, for I never fully realized why the wondrous sword was so light that I could carry it, yet it was so large that nine hands together could hold the hilt of it.

I returned from the mountain to the City of Onai. In the fields outside the city I saw an old woman stand up and shade her eyes to look at me a'coming. Soon all stopped their labors. Carts stopped. Donkeys squealed. Everything became quiet. When the people ran up to look upon my countenance, they must have been persuaded because every one of them took up his meager tool and followed me into the city.

We destroyed Onai because the Atlatians spat in my eye when I demanded they open the granaries to feed our people. So unprepared were the Atlatians for this that they were easily overtaken, for they did not know of battle.

I opened the granaries to our poor people, and then we burned Onai to the ground. It never occurred to me that I couldn't do that, for I did not care if I lived or died at that point; I had nothing left to live for.

When the slaughter and burning were finished, a great hurt was still within my being, for my hatred had not been satisfied. So I ran from the people to hide in the hills, but they followed me in spite of all my cursing and throwing stones and spitting at them.

"Ram, Ram, Ram, Ram," they chanted, carrying their tools of the field and grain tied in linens, and herding sheep and goats before them. I shouted at the people to leave me alone and go home. But still they came, for they no longer had a home. I was their home.

Since they insisted on following after me wherever I went, I gathered together all these soulless creatures of different denominations, and they became my army, my people. And great people were they indeed. But soldiers? Hardly. But from then on, the great army of the Ram assembled itself. Its number in the beginning was close to ten thousand.

From that time I was a driven entity, a barbarian, who despised the tyranny of men. I hated man and fought, fully expecting to die. I did not have the fear of dying that many of my people did because I wanted to die honorably. I never knew fear. I only knew hate.

When you lead a charge and you are the one in front, with no one on either side of you, you have to be crazy. A person who would do that is filled with a powerful drive called hate. So I was very much a spectacle to be hewed down by the noblest of foe, if they would only do me the honor. And I picked the worthiest opponents to be my demise. But, you know, when there is an absence of fear, there is a presence of conquering. Thus I became a great conqueror. Before my time there was no such thing as a conqueror, only tyrants.

I created war. I was the first conqueror this plane ever knew. Until my time there was no warring faction against the arrogance of the Atlatians. None. I created it. In my anger and hostility and my desire to be noble and honorable to what I felt, I became what you would term a great entity. Know you what a hero is? Well, I was one indeed. The hero salvages life and puts an end to the wrongs of life, not realizing that in doing so, he is also creating a wrong. I desired to do away with all forms of tyranny and I did, only to become the very thing I despised.

Thereafter I was driven to slay tyranny and to make the color of my skin more respectable. And from all the sieges and battles we put forth — the lands that we crossed and all the people we freed along the way — one by one my army grew, and great became the legend of the Ram and his army.

I was an imbecile, a barbarian, a buffoon, an ignorant entity of savage acclaim. And for ten years into my march, I warred upon innocents and hacked and burned my way across many lands until I was run through with a great sword. Had they left it in me, I might have been all right, but they pulled it out to make sure that I would bleed to death. I saw the river of life ebbing from my being onto a snowy, marbled floor that seemingly was perfect, only to see that the river of scarlet had found a crack in it.

As I lay there on the cold, marble floor, watching the blood issue forth from my being, there came a voice. It spoke to me and it said, "Stand up." It said, "Stand up."

I pulled up my head and put forth my palms. Then I began to pull under me the knees of my being. As I raised my countenance so that my head was erect and even, I pulled up my left foot and stabilized it. Then gathering all of my strength, I put my hand upon my knee, my fist into my wound, and I stood up.

As I stood there — with blood issuing from my mouth, flowing through my fingers, and running down my legs — my assailants, who were now certain that I was immortal, fled from me. My soldiers laid siege to the city and burned it to the ground.

I would never forget the voice that made me stand up, that kept me from dying. In the years to come I would seek to find the face of that voice.

I was given to the court of women in my march to be cared for. And I had to endure the stinking poultices of vulture grease that were put upon my chest. I had to be bossed by the women and undressed before their eyes. I could not even urinate or spill dung from my anus in private but had to do it in front of them, a most humiliating experience. I have acclaimed even to this day that the vulture grease was not to heal me but was so wretched that when I breathed it, it kept life in me. During my healing, much of my pride and hate had to give way to survival.

While I was recovering from my ghastly wound and couldn't do anything else, I began to contemplate everything around me. One day I watched an old woman pass from this plane, clutching heartily the crudely woven linen she had made for her son who had perished long ago. I saw the woman pass in the light of the noonday sun, life ebbing from her body in choking strokes of weeping. As I watched the old woman shrivel in the light, her mouth opened to an aghast expression and her eyes became glazed, unaffected by the light. Nothing moved, save the breeze and her old hair.

I thought about the woman and her son who had perished, and I thought about their great intelligence. Then I looked back at the sun, which never perished. It was the very same sun the old woman had seen through a crack in the roof of her hovel when she first opened her eyes as a babe, and it was the last thing she saw when she died.

I looked again at the sun. You know, it was oblivious that she had died. I watched it as we buried the old woman under a tall poplar tree by the river.

As the sun set that evening, I cursed it. I watched it sit upon the mantel of the mountains like a great fiery jewel, scarlet-eyed. I looked upon the purpled mountains and the valley, already shrouded in mist, and saw rods of the sun's light gild all things and make them illusionarily beautiful. I saw clouds, once the pallor of blue, become vividly alive in hues of scarlet, fire-rose, and pink.

I continued to watch the great light as it retired behind the mountains, now looming like piercing teeth on the horizon, until the last rods of its beauty had descended behind the last mount. I heard a night bird cry above me, and I looked into the heavens to see the pale moon waxing against a darkening sky. A breeze came up and, as it blew my hair and dried my tears, it made me sick in my being.

You know, I was a great warrior. With a sword I could cleave a man in half in a moment. I had beheaded, hacked, and butchered. I had smelled blood and burned people. But why did I do all of that? The sun set in its magnificence anyway. The bird cried in the night anyway. And the moon came up in spite of it all.

That is when I began to ponder the Unknown God. The only thing I truly wanted was to understand that which seemed so awesome, so mysterious, and so very far away. And what was man? What was he? Why was he not greater than the sun? Why couldn't the old woman live? Why was man — though the teeming multitude upon the plane, the creating force, the unifying force — the most vulnerable of all creation? If man was so important, as my people told me, why wasn't he important enough that when he died, the sun stood still to mourn his passing, or the moon turned purple, or the fowl ceased to fly? Man was very unimportant, it seemed, for all these things continued in spite of his peril.

All I wanted was to know.

I did not have a teacher to teach me of the Unknown God, for I did not trust any man. I had seen and lost so much through the wickedness of man and his altered thinking. I had seen man despise man and think him to be soulless. I had seen innocents gutted and burned out of fear. I had seen children, naked on slave blocks, examined by perverted souls who plucked from them their hairs of adolescence so they would still have the image of young children as they were raped. I had seen priests and prophets invent, through their hatred for mankind, creatures of great torment and ugliness so they could govern and enslave people through the rule of religious forms.

There was no man living that I would have as my teacher, for any man living had altered thinking, had taken that which was really pure and innocent and altered it through his own limited understanding. So I wanted nothing to do with a God created through man's understanding, for if man created the God, the God was fallible.

It was life's elements, the truest teachers of all, that taught me of the Unknown God. I learned from days. I learned from nights. I learned from tender, insignificant life that abounded even in the face of destruction and war.

I contemplated the sun in its advent of glory upon the horizon. I watched its journey through the heavens, ending up in the western sphere and passing into its sleep. I learned that the sun, though mute, subtly controlled life, for all who were brave and gallant and warring with one another ceased their warring when the sun went down.

I watched the beauty of the moon in her pale light as she danced across the heavens, illuminating the darkness in mysterious and wonderful ways. I saw the fires from our encampment and how they lit up the evening sky. I listened to the wildfowl landing on the water, birds rustling in their night nest, and children and their laughter. I observed falling stars, nightingales, the frost on the reeds, and the lake slivered with ice to create the illusion of another world. I saw the leaves of olive trees turn from emerald to silver as the wind blew through them.

I observed women standing in the river as they gathered water in their urns, their clothing tied up in knots to reveal their alabaster knees. I listened to the clatter of the women's gossip and the teasing in their laughter. I smelled the smoke from distant fires and the garlic and wine on the breath of my men.

It was not until I observed and pondered life and its

ongoingness that I discovered who the Unknown God truly was. I reasoned that the Unknown God was not the Gods created through the altered thinking of man. I realized that the Gods in men's minds are only the personalities of the things they fear and respect the most; that the true God is the ongoing essence that permits man to create and play out his illusions, however he chooses, and that will still be there when man returns yet again another spring, another life. I realized that it is in the power and the ongoingness of the life force where the Unknown God truly lies.

Who was the Unknown God? It was me, and the birds in their night nest, the frost on the reeds, the morning dawn, and evening sky. It was the sun and the moon, children and their laughter, alabaster knees and running water, and the smell of garlic and leather and brass. This understanding took a long time for me to grasp, though it had been right in front of me all the time. The Unknown God wasn't beyond the moon or the sun. It was all around me. And with this new birth of reasoning, I began to embrace life, to hold that dear to me, and to find a reason to live. There was more than blood and death and the stench of war. There was life, far greater than we had ever perceived it to be.

It was through this realization that I would understand in the years to come that man is the greatest of all things; that the only reason the sun is ongoing, while man dies, is the sun never even contemplates death. All it knows is to be.

When I realized through contemplative thought who the Unknown God was and what it was, I did not wish to wither and die, as the old woman had died. There must be a way, I thought, to be as ongoing as the sun.

Once I had healed from the dire wound to my body, I had little to do but to sit upon a plateau and watch my army grow fat and lazy. One day as I looked to the horizon to see the vague outline of ghostly mountains and valleys yet uncharted, I wondered what would it be like to be the Unknown God, the life element; how could I be part of this essence that is ongoing.

That is when the wind played a jest upon me and insulted me beyond my means. It blew up my cloak, which was long and regal, and dumped it on top of my head, a most embarrassing thing. Not a very noble position for a conqueror. Then the wind caused a wonderful pillar of saffron-colored dust to form a column beside me all the way up into the heavens. Then when I was not paying enough attention, the wind ceased, allowing all the dust to fall upon me.

Then the wind went whistling down the canyon, down to where the river flowed, and on through the wonderful olive orchards, turning the leaves from emerald to silver. And it blew a beautiful maiden's skirt up around her waist, with all the giggling that went on from that. And then it blew the hat from a little child's head and the child went racing after it, laughing gleefully.

I demanded that the wind come back to me, but it only laughed in its gales in the canyon. Then when I was blue in the face from shouting orders, I sat back down upon my haunches and it came and blew in my face softly. That is freedom.

While there was no man I would have as my ideal, the wind performed itself to be very much an ideal for me. You cannot see the wind, yet when it comes upon you in a fury, you are assailed. And no matter how grand and powerful you are, you cannot declare war upon the wind. What can you do to it? Cleave it with your broadsword? Hack it with your ax? Spit upon it? It will only throw it back in your face.

What else could man be, I thought, that would give him such free movement, such power; that could never be captivated by the limited nature of man; that would permit him to be in all places at all times and, unlike man, never dies?

To me the wind was an ultimate essence, for it is ongoing, free-moving, all-consuming. It has no boundaries and no form. It is magical, exploratory, and adventurous, and that indeed is the closest resemblance there is to the God essence of life. And the wind never judges man. The wind never forsakes man. The wind, if you call it, will come to you through love. Ideals should be like that.

So I desired to become the wind. And I contemplated on it for years and years. That became my ideal. That was what I wanted to be. That was what all my thoughts were bent on becoming. I contemplated the wind and aligned myself with its elusiveness and lightness and contours that are indefinable. And as I contemplated the wind, it was the wind that I became in my search for becoming.

The first occurrence was not until six years after I had been run through. Every evening I would go and sit upon my solitary plateau, gaze into the moon with her soft pallor, and contemplate the wind. And there came a time, much to my surprise, when I found myself aloft in the heavens and did not know who I was when I turned to look down.

In but a moment I realized that I was far away from my simple speck of a body down on the plateau. When I looked down upon my embodiment, I felt fear for the first time since I was run through. It was fear that brought me back to the body.

I opened my eyes to a cold/hot sweat over the realization that I had been elsewhere, outside of the prison of my embodiment. I was in paradise because I was sure that I had become the wind. I flung myself to the ground and praised God: the Source, the Power, the Cause, the Wind. I would never forget that splendid moment when I became the grace and beauty and bountiful life of the wind. And I reasoned that what allowed me to become that was my complete determination to become my ideal, always holding clear in thought the vision of what I wanted to become.

The next eve I went to my place of solitary movement, contemplated the wind with exuberant joy, and I became nothing. I tried again and again and again. I knew that my experience was not simply my imagination. I had seen a different perspective. I had been in the air as a dove or a hawk and had seen my pitiful self below me.

Nothing did I want, nothing did I desire — nothing —except the one thought of becoming that freedom. But no matter how hard I struggled and how much sweat broke out upon my body and how much cursing followed thereafter, I didn't go anywhere. I stayed — and much heavier than before — because I had become more aware, mind you, of how heavy I was. But I never lost sight of my ideal, nor did I ever forget that moment of feeling when I first looked down upon my pitiful body.

It was a long time before I became the wind again, two years in your time-reckoning from the first event. This time it happened not upon contemplating the wind but upon going into a restful sleep. I had praised the Source, the sun, life, saffron dust, the moon, the stars, the sweet smells of jasmine. I praised them all. And ere I closed my lids, I was in the heavens again as the wind.

Once I had perfected my ability to leave my body, it took me a long time to reckon how to go places. Then it happened one day that one of my men came into a most perilous position. He had fallen from his horse with his foot still lodged in a stirrup. The moment I put my thought with him, I was with him, and I released his heel. I stood over him and wished him well, but he thought I was a dream.

For many years I traveled in thought into other kingdoms and to other entities. I visited civilizations in the birth of their future and lives yet unseen. I learned to travel in moments, for I learned that wherever the thought is, so is the entity. And how did I conquer thereafter? I was an awesome foe, for I knew my enemies' thinking; thus I outwitted them all. No longer did I besiege kingdoms; I let them besiege themselves.

Slowly over many years — as the thought of becoming my ideal became the very life force in the cells of my embodiment — my soul gradually changed the programming in every cellular structure to increase the vibratory rate within them, my desire was that strong. The more peaceful I became with life, the more that emotion carried through my entire physical arrangement until I became lighter and lighter and lighter. People would look at me and say, "Alas, there is a glow about the master." There was, for my body was vibrating at a faster rate of speed, going from the speed of matter into the speed of light. That is what emanated a glow from my being.

In time my body became fainter and fainter by the light of the moon. Then one night I became where the moon was. No longer did I simply travel in thought. I had raised my bodily vibrations into light and had taken my entire embodiment with me. I was gleeful and mirthful, for that which I had done was unheard of. Yet I came back, but only to see if I could to it again. And I did, again and again and again, sixty-three times before my final ascension. It became an expectancy, as breathing is to you.

When I became the wind, I realized how truly limited I had been and how free the elements were. When I became the wind, I became an unseen power that has no form, that is pulsating light, indivisible. In that, I could move with freedom through valleys and dales and glens, through mountains and oceans and stratums, and none could see me. And, like the wind, I had the power to turn leaves from emerald to silver, to move trees that are unshakable, to go into the lungs of a babe, into the mouth of a lover, and back into the clouds to push them away. When I became the wind, I became the height of a moving power that can never be tamed, a wild movement that is free: free of weight, free of measure, free of time.

When I became the wind, I realized how small and helpless man is in his ignorance about himself and how great he becomes when he extends himself into knowledge. I learned that whatever man contemplates long enough, merely by desire he will become. If man tells himself long enough that he is wretched, soulless, powerless, he will believe it and become it. If he calls himself lord of the wind, he will be lord of the wind, as I became lord of the wind. And if he calls himself God, he is going to become God.

Once I had learned these things, I began to teach my beloved brothers about the Unknown God, the Source of all life. There came a day when I was an old man, when all I had set out to accomplish in my being had been accomplished. I made a journey across the River Indus and there, on the side of the mountain called Indus, I communed with all of my people for one hundred and twenty days. I urged them to know that these understandings were a truth, that the source of their divine guidance was not through me or any other man but through the God that had created us all. For their belief — and to their surprise — I elevated myself quite nicely above them. Women screamed and became aghast.

Soldiers dropped their broadswords in wonderment. I saluted them all farewell and urged them to learn as I had learned, to become as I had become in their own way.

Through learning how to comprehend life elements that I found more forceful than man — elements that I found more intelligent than man, that live in a peaceful coexistence beside and in spite of man — did I discover the Unknown God.

If you ask man, "How should I look? What should I believe in? How should I live?" — if you do that, you will die. That is a truth. Go and ask the wind: "Give me knowledge, wind. Open me up and let me know," and it will turn you from olive to silver and take you into the hollows of the canyons and laugh with you blatantly free.

I was most fortunate in being taught by life's elements. The sun never cursed me and the moon never said I must be a certain way. And the elements never reflected failure to me. The frost and the dew, the smell of grass, the insects going to and fro, the cry of the nighthawk, they are all unfailing things whose essence is simple. And a wonderful thing about them, in their simplicity and steadfastness: They asked nothing of me. The sun did not look down and say, "Ramtha, you must worship me in order to know me." The moon did not look down and say, "Ramtha, wake up. It is time to look upon my beauty." They were there whenever I looked to see them.

I learned from something that is constant, without judgment, and easily understood if a man puts his mind to it. Because of that, I was not at the hands of the altered thinking of man with his hypocrisy, dogma, superstitious beliefs, and multifaceted Gods that you must try to appease. That is why it was easy for me to learn in one existence on this plane what most have yet to understand because they look for God in another man's understanding. They look for God in governmental rule, in church rule, in a history which they have yet to question who wrote it or why it was written. Man has based his beliefs, his understandings, his thought processes, his lives on something that life after life after life has proven itself a failure. Yet man, stumbling over his own altered thinking, imprisoned by his own arrogance, continues the steadfast hypocrisy that only leads to death.

After I ascended is when I knew everything I wanted to know because I went out of the density of flesh and into the fluidness of thought and, in so doing, I was not inhibited by anything. Then I knew that man truly was, in his essence, God. Before I ascended I did not know there was such a thing as a soul, nor did I understand the mechanics of ascending the embodiment. I only knew that I was at peace with what I had done and I was at peace with life. I was no longer an ignorant barbarian anxious for battle. I was no longer overwrought and overworked. I embraced life and the wonderfulness that I saw in the heavens day after day and night after night. That was my life.

I learned to love myself when I compared myself with something great and majestic. My life became fulfilled when I took hold of all my understanding and focused it on myself. That is when peace came. That is when I began to know more. That is when I became one with the Unknown God.

It was not the wind that I became but the ideal that the wind represented to me. I am now the lord over it, for I became the unseen principle that is free and omnipresent and one with all life. It was when I became that principle that I understood the Unknown God and all that it is — and all that it isn't — because that is what I wanted to understand. I found the answers within me that allowed me to expand into a grander understanding.

I was Ram the Conqueror. I am now Ram the God. I was a barbarian who became God through the simplest and yet the most profound of things. What I teach you is what I learned.

***

CHAPTER 3

When You Were My People

*For those of you who worship, that is your choice to
be lost for lifetimes in another's identity.*

When many of you were my people long ago, we crossed
great continents together and laid siege on notorious tyrants. And
through all the heavy battles — long marches, unknown countries,
threatening seas and blistering storms — did all of you gain the
prize of freedom, a freedom that you had at the end of the march
only because you had crossed the borders of your greatest terrors
and were still alive to reach a new homeland. When you reached
it, so fearless were you, so courageous were you, so tired were
you, that home became the planting of seeds in the fields, the
harvesting of food, and the raising of children and animals because
peace is the result when one has conquered his greatest fears. So
all that you had gained by the end of your march was well worth
the journey, far away from your homeland, into a new dimension
of understanding.

When I was ready to leave, you were planting your seeds
and having your children, building your hovels and plowing the
land, enjoying good food and a sweet morning and a peaceful
night. That was your destiny, for that was your desire fulfilled.
That was your reward.

You were bedding your new lives, and it was time for me
to go to my life, for what you were gaining in your understanding
of peace was only contentment to me. But that which I was going

to, which was my home, was the great, elusive Unknown God, the grand mystery that caused all things to occur.

The morning of my leaving was a wondrous day and a grand but short farewell. You had little ones to care for, fields to tend, and cattle to look after. And I, I went unto my Father, whom I sought after all my life and found in a wondrous place of understanding. That indeed was my destiny because I desired no other destiny.

Each of you has returned to live here life after life after life, and through each of those lives you have gained and progressed greatly in your understanding. Now many of you are wanting to know. Now you are searching for the understanding that I hungered for and found. You have had your homes. You have passed your valuable seed on to the world. You have had all the learnings, all the experiences. Now you are ready to learn what you could not learn before because your priorities were different then. So for the love of you and all mankind have I come back to teach you, as I promised I would long, long ago. And I will teach you as a grand teacher indeed, but I expect you to do only what you feel is right; that is all.

I have not returned to tell you of the splendor that lies beyond this place but to help you see it for yourselves, and not through philosophical understandings but through teachings that ring so blatantly true within you that your soul urges you to become the divine principle you had forgotten long ago. And for you to continue as a race of entities in this form, it is most important that you learn of your own divinity as well as everyone else's. Through the power of my being and for the love of your being, I will teach you, as I taught myself, how to return to your greatness and your glory. And in your joy, I will laugh with you. And when you weep, I will send a wind to dry your tears.

Through this teaching you will learn to become the sovereign that you were in all your glory when you began this remarkable journey. You will learn to listen solely to the voice within you and to follow only the path of joy. You will learn how to feel profoundly so that you gain the truest treasure of this plane: emotion. And you will come to love yourself so grandly that no matter who stands before you, you will find God in them as you have found it in yourself, and you will love them as deeply as you have learned to love yourself. Then you who have taught yourself so eloquently will be a brilliant light to the world, only because you are a radiant example of the love of self.

Now this teaching is not a religious understanding, for religion is dogmatic, restrictive, and very judgmental. I am not a teacher of religion, for it has brought great division and great hurt to this plane. This teaching is simply knowledge. It is learning; it is experience; it is love. I will love you into knowing God and becoming the unlimitedness that God is.

This teaching is lawless. It possesses no laws, for law is a limitation that obstructs freedom. I will teach you of nothing but God and options. I am here to open the doors to greater knowledge so that you realize your options for living upon this plane; so you realize that your life is not limited to this plane, for life exists on other planes and in many other places.

I am here to help you who are enslaved by fear, entrapped by your own thought processes, to begin to see a new vista of unlimited thinking, unlimited purpose, unlimited life. That I will teach you this day, to whatever point you want to receive it, to whatever point you wish to live it. I am going to lead you from your cloistered self back into your own greatness. And that which is within you, which is called the lamp within, shall be lit brighter.

I ask of you nothing other than to be yourself. But most here do not know who self is. I will teach you how to find it again and, when found, you will never let go of it again. Then no one will need to teach you thereafter. Then you are sovereign in your own truth and free to live according to your own designs.

I have chosen to come back to you through the embodiment of a woman who was my beloved daughter in my times. When I was upon your plane, I married not any woman. But on my march many entities gave me their children as a gift of appreciation. There were cheesemakers who gave me cheese and winemakers who gave me wine. And there were those whose greatest prize was their children, and they gave them to the House of Ram. For an entity who had never lain with a woman, I had more children than anyone I knew. And the children were great teachers for me for, in their innocence and purity of Spirit, children live a very simple truth.

My daughter was one of these children, and this child I loved greatly. The little girl did not want to be a little girl; she wanted to be a warrior. Being a woman and weaving and doing womanish things did not appeal to her. She never really understood war until a long time later. But the entity loved me dearly. And she wanted nothing more than to learn, and that I admired.

On the day of my ascension I promised my daughter that I would return, though she knew not where I was going. I charged her to go to the land called Turk, where she lived out her days waiting for me to come back. I never did.

My daughter has lived many lives and has been burned and beheaded and starved for what she knew to be a truth. Through all of those lives she has emerged to be a noble creature who lives what she is humbly. It is because of that humility that I have been able to return through her to remind her of the heritage that she and you forgot long ago. This is her service to the world. And to her, as to you, I have fulfilled my word.

I came to my daughter in the midst of her life at a time when such unexpected things do not occur. Because she was prim and proper and innocent, and did not venture into extraordinary beliefs, I chose her for this service and taught her for a long time what I am teaching you. Through knowledge and learning we began this work together, at first to be unannounced in your marketplace in order that it might grow one by one.

I have chosen to speak with you in this fashion because you are all prone to worship the images of others and exalt them above yourselves. So for those who come into my audience, I have no body to worship nor feet to kiss. And my daughter will not allow you to do it to hers, for they are her feet, after all. When you leave my audience, you will have no image by which you can remember me — and no picture that you can dangle around your neck, put upon your wall, or carve into stone — for what is being taught here is not to worship me but to wholly worship and love what you are and this wonderful essence that lies latent within you called God Almighty.

I am no different than you are. There is no one, seen or unseen, who can ever be greater than you, and there is no one who can ever be less than you. All are equal in the kingdom of God.

Those of you who desire to follow and worship, or to do more outside of yourselves than within yourselves, I wish you to know that I am not what you are searching for. I am here to help you become sovereign in your own truth, in your own understanding. As long as you serve or worship or devote yourselves to anything outside of yourselves, you will never express the sublime beauty that you are, nor will you ever become truly free.

Only you can be your greatest lover. Only you can be your greatest friend and teacher. There is no voice that will ever teach you greater than your own. There is no word written that will ever teach you greater than your own. Who you are this day is the answer to everything you have ever wanted. But if you insist on looking outside of yourselves for paths to follow and entities to worship, you will never truly see or know the glory of God. You can only realize your divinity, your enlightenment, your unfoldment through yourself and your proclaimed love of self. The only way to peace and happiness and fulfillment in your life is to worship and love yourself — for that is loving God — and to love yourself greater than anyone else, for that is what will give you the love and steadfastness to embrace the whole of humanity.

So I, Ramtha, am not the standard from which to draw your ideal. You cannot understand the mystery of yourself through me, only through knowledge. The purpose of this teaching is to instill through knowledge and experience a steadfast knowingness within you who will seek out the Unknown God and realize it is yourself. And that is your journey — and yours alone — for it is your life and yours alone. Teacher I am, splendid; but the ideal I am not. That you have made your way to this teaching I am indeed pleased, but you shall not linger here.

Whatever I teach you, whatever you learn, so shall it

manifest into your life. Then you will know that what is being taught here is not a philosophy but an absolute truth. And from each manifestation you will grow and become stronger and more light and more quiet and more simple. And in that simplicity you will find the wind, and that power and that source will uplift you.

All of you have been governed entities, and your governess has been fear. It has always been. Knowledge permits you to do away with fear so that you are no longer enslaved by another's wishes but can live wholly in the freedom of your own. When you have knowledge, you will always be free — always. The more you contemplate, apply, and experience these teachings, the freer and more joyful you will become.

One day — whether in this life or in those that follow — when the marketplace no longer offers you any more, there will be a great emptiness, a great pull, and a great desire to become all. Then you too will look forward to every moment on the plateau, for there the wind is like strong fingers in your hair. Birds are taking flight to far-off nesting places, and the sun is brilliant with golden rods across your heavens. And when you do as I did and become — for that is the most important thing to you — I will welcome you where Ram went, for the door to freedom, called knowledge, is there for you who will open your thought processes to a grander understanding and then live that understanding not outside of you but inside of you. When you have lived it, then you are finished here; then you are off to a new adventure. And the adventures that lie beyond this place are grander and more spectacular than you can imagine. So pliable are you in light that you can travel to outer space or to inner space, wherever you desire to go.

I love you deeply. If I did not, I could not come to you in the way that I have. When you learn to love yourself as I love you, you will understand these truths and you will understand the greatness that you truly are. And that shall be a grand and glorious day.

***

CHAPTER 4

God Is

God loves you with greater love than you have ever fathomed,
for it is the life that you are, the ground that you walk on,
the air that you breathe.

My beloved brothers, many of you have been taught for ages that the essence called God is a somber, fearsome, angry, judgmental character. But God is none of these things. The God who harangues, who judges, who persecutes, has never existed except in the hearts and minds of men. It is man who created a God that judges some and exalts others. That is a God of man, the creation of man and his will.

The God that I know, that I love, that is the power that issues forth from me and the kingdom that I am, is a God of complete and unjudgmental love. It is nothing else but everything else. God loves you with greater love than you have ever fathomed, for it is the life that you are, the ground that you walk on, the air that you breathe. It is the color of your skin, the magnificence of your eyes, the gentleness of your touch. It is you in every moment that you are, in every thought that you think, in every deed that you do, even in the shadows of your soul.

God is an all-consuming force that is everything. It is the wind upon the water, the changing of leaves, the simplicity of a rose deep in its color and hue. God is lovers in their embrace, children in their laughter, and the sheen of honey-colored hair. It is the sun rising in the morning, a star twinkling in the night, the moon waxing and waning across the midnight sky. God is the beauteous insect, the humble bird in flight, the vile and ugly worm. God is movement and color, sound and light. God is passion. God is love. God is joy. God is sadness. That which is — all that is — is what you term God the Father, the totality of life, and the lover of all that it is.

God is not a singular character who sits upon a throne and judges the whole of life. God is the whole of life, every pulsating moment. It is the ongoingness and foreverness of everything that is.

Do you think that you have been judged by life? Not at all, for if God — which is what you are — were to judge you, it would certainly be judging itself. And why would the supreme intelligence do that?

The life force that you term the Father does not even have the ability to judge you or any other thing, for life does not possess a personality with an ego that can divide itself into facets of good and evil, right and wrong, perfect and imperfect. If God possessed an ego, it would also possess the ability to perceive alteredness within itself. And if God could contemplate alteredness within its being, even for one moment, then the life that God is would cease in the next moment and it would never be again.

God of itself is wholly without goodness or evil. It is wholly without positive or negative. God is not perfect, for perfection is a limitation to ongoing, ever-changing, exuberant life. God simply is. The only thing that your beloved Father knows how to do is to be, so that everything — which is him — can express the life that it is.

God is unlimited, supreme beingness, an undivided totality of Isness. And that Isness loves you so grandly that it has allowed you to create the illusions of perfection and imperfection, good and evil, positive and negative. And through your perception it has become what you have perceived. Thus God, being the totality of all that is, is the wrong as well as the right; it is the ugliness as well as the beauty; it is the vileness as well as the divinity.

The Father has never judged you in this or any moment you have ever lived. He has been you and the platform of life upon which you have expressed your own divine, purposeful self.

He has given you the uniqueness of your own ego and the freedom of will to become whatever you wish to become, to perceive the life that he is, however you choose to perceive it. And nothing you have ever done, nothing you have ever thought — no matter how vile or wretched or wonderful it has been — has ever been seen by God as anything other than being.

This God that I know loves you with greater, more profound love than you have ever conceived of, for it has allowed you to create your life however you have desired. The Father has always loved you. He knows of no other way to perceive you, for that which you are is he.

The Father sees no wrong; he sees only himself. The Father sees no failure; he sees only his Isness ongoing into forever. You create the blossoms of life and even the vileness of it, and the Father will become the vileness and the blossoms and yet never judge the two as to which is greater or which is less. He simply is. He is the Isness that allows you to express through him however you choose. And it is a good thing he is that way, for if he truly were this God created by man, there is not one of you who would ever see what is called pearled gates — not one of you — for there is not one of you who could ever live up to the expectations of this God created by man.

Only you, through your own attitudes and the acceptance of the attitudes of others, have ever judged yourself. Only you have ever caused yourself to feel failure. With the ability to create from your Father whatever truth and reality you desire, you are the sole judge of your own life. Only you have ever determined what is good and what is bad, what is right and what is wrong. Yet in the Isness called life, no thing is any of these. Everything simply is a part of the Isness that is called God Almighty. Your judgment is only an illusion that you have created upon this plane of creative realities.

In your limited thinking, you have thought that some things are wrong, that they are evil. But that has been your selection of truth, and the Father has allowed you to have it. His truth is called Isness. God loves you regardless of what you do because everything you do or think enhances the life that he is through the wisdom that you gain from it. God knows that you are forever and that nothing you do can ever take your life force from you. So when you pass from this plane and you ponder all the things you have done in your life — and you will — God will still be there loving you into all of your tomorrows, for he is the platform through which you create your illusions, your imagination, your dreams.

Now what is God in its most exalted form? Thought. The Father — the platform from which you create your life, the substance and life force of all things — is, in a greater understanding, thought, for thought is the ultimate creator of all things that are, that ever have been, that ever will be. Thought is the substance from which all things are created. Everything that is has come forth first from thought, which is the supreme intelligence called the mind of God.

Have you ever pondered what holds all things together in their unique patterns and forms? It is thought, which is the cosmic glue called love. That is what holds all matter together. That is love on the grandest scale of all, for that is what the Father is. Everything — even your body — is held together by thought, for everything has been envisioned through thought, which is God, and it is the Father's love of himself that holds everything in place.

You are held together by God. What allows all the molecular and cellular structures of your body to cling together is the love of the grand and magnificent thought that God truly is. Without thought, your body would not exist, matter would not exist, nothing would exist, for thought is the creator and supportive element of all life.

Do you think that God — the thought that holds and binds all things together — is a somber and fearsome entity? It is not. The Father is complete joy, for he knows of no other way to be. He is all life forms vibrating in harmony with one another, which emits a tone that sounds like the roar of laughter. If you listen carefully, you can even hear the music of the Father, the laughter of God. It is most joyous. I have not once heard him weep.

So what is God, the cause of your precious being, the wondrous life force that flows and ebbs amongst all of you, that connects and binds you together, that is the promise of life hereafter and eternities to come? It is the Isness that is thought. It is the Isness of ongoing life. It is the Isness that loves all that it is. It is the Isness that allows life to be through love. It is the Isness that is complete and utter joy. That is your heritage and your destiny.

Student: You have taught that God is simply an Isness. And you use many terms besides the term God to refer to this life-force intelligence. But why do you often choose to use the words "he" and "Father"? That seems to perpetuate the notion that God is not only an identity outside of us but a male character, and that seems a bit offensive to some women.

Ramtha: To educate the whole of humanity, one must utilize the different terms which have been used to describe God; that is, one must refer to the Isness in ways that all can relate to. Though the Isness has been referred to as the Father and thus thought of as a male gender, the Father is not a man; yet man in his gender is the Father. But so be woman, for the Father is both male and female.

The term God is sexless. It means supreme intelligence. Those who do not understand the term Isness need to know the word Father. Those who do not understand supreme intelligence need to know the word God.

Master, if one insists that God is a Father, that is his truth. If there are women who are outraged because someone has called God a male gender, then that is their truth. But God will always be the perception of what God is, and that will always be unique for each entity.

God is not a word. It is a feeling that lives within each of us. And the more unlimited your perception of God, the grander and more joyful that feeling will be as it encompasses more of the emotion called God Almighty.

Ramtha: (To an elderly woman in a wheelchair) Dear lady, who rides on silver wheels, what say you?

Student: I love God, but I'm afraid of dying.

Ramtha: Why?

Student: I don't know. I can't reach the bottom of it. I've thought of it and thought of it and thought of it.

Ramtha: Do you believe in hell?

Student: Yes, I do.

Ramtha: That is why you don't want to die, for that is where you feel you are going.

Student: Oh, well, I don't think I'm going. I don't believe God will let me go because I've asked for forgiveness for all the wrongs I've done.

Ramtha: My lady, my lady. Do you believe that the Father has less love for you than you do for your own children?

Student: No. Well, I just don't feel like he loves me sometimes. Maybe I feel that maybe I'm not forgiven. But still I know I am.

Ramtha: What have you done that is so wrong?

Student: Well, several things.

Ramtha: Have those several things kept you from living?

Student: No. I have tried to live, and I want to live and I want to live right.

Ramtha: And what does that mean?

Student: That means the devil won't get me.

Ramtha: Indeed?

Student: Well, you tell me, please, what it is.

Ramtha: Would you believe me if I did?

Student: I will.

Ramtha: What if I told you there is no hell?

Student: But I've been taught that there is a hell though.

Ramtha: But I'm teaching you there isn't. Will you believe me as firmly as you have believed that there is a hell?

Student: Well, I believe you.

Ramtha: Then accept it, for there isn't.

Do you know what hell is? It is a term that was used in the kingdom of Judea to describe a shallow, open grave where an entity would be put because he could not afford the drachmas or the shekels to be entombed. And it was a damnation to have a shallow grave because at night the hyenas and wild dogs would dig up the body and devour it. And because the embodiment was devoured, entities believed that they could never go on to their utopia. That is all the term ever meant until a later translation, when preachers and priests and religion determined it to be a place of torment.

Student: Well, I read my Bible regularly, and it puts emphasis on hell.

Ramtha: Who wrote the Bible?

Student: Different ones.

Ramtha: Who were they? Were they men?

Student: I don't know.

Ramtha: They were.

I have looked into the depths of your world, into the center, to find a burning lake of fire, and it was not there. I went to the farthest reaches of your universe to find a place of torment, and it was not there either. And I looked in the same places for a devil and could find him nowhere. And when I returned, I found him in the hearts of those who believe in him and in hell. But there is no such place.

Student: Well, I'm glad you think so.

Ramtha: I don't think so. I know so.

Student: You know, it doesn't seem like God would love us so much and then for the least little thing we did, he would send us to hell to live in burning fire.

Ramtha: That is precisely correct. The Father has not created any such place to torment anyone, for were you not created by God?

Student: Yes.

Ramtha: Then since you were created by God, do you not have God in you?

Student: I have God in me. I love God.

Ramtha: But are you not part of God?

Student: Am I?

Ramtha: Indeed.

Student: Well, that means a lot to me.

Ramtha: My lady, since God is everything, what would he make you out of if he didn't make you out of himself? You are God. So why would he ever cast himself into a pit and not love himself for doing what is called a wrong that is also a part of the life that he is?

I will tell you a great truth: Man has created images of God that he could use to control his brothers. Religions were created to control people and nations when armies failed, and fear was the tool that kept them in line. If you take the divinity out of any man — take God out of him — then you can easily rule and control him.

God has not created a hell or a devil. Those were dreadful creations of man to torment his brothers. They were created through religious dogma for the purpose of intimidating the masses into a controllable organization. That is a great truth.

God the Father is everything, every little grain of sand in the sea, every butterfly in spring, every great and small star in the vastness of your heavens. All things are God. So for him to have a place such as hell would be like a cancer in his body, and it would eat him up.

There is nothing that will ever take you from the kingdom of heaven, for there is nothing greater than God and life. God the Father is forever loving you because he is every direction you turn, every thought you embrace.

Student: God loves all of us. I know he does.

Ramtha: Indeed, indeed, for he is all of us. And what about all of your wrongs? My wondrous lady, you have done nothing wrong. Nothing.

Student: Why, thank you.

Ramtha: For life has not been altered because of anything you have done. Everything you have ever done, however vile or wretched it has been, has enhanced life by the wisdom you have obtained from doing it.

Now I wish you to understand this: Your religion and your belief have caused the annihilation of civilizations for ages. Your Mayans and Aztecs were obliterated and murdered through the rule of the church because they did not believe as the church did. All of the holy wars in your Dark Ages were fought to further religious beliefs. And in a place called France, babes were plucked from their mothers' arms because they did not believe according to the church. Women had their eyes burned out with hot irons and their chests branded, and the streets ran with blood, all because of a belief.

Then the Protestants took what is called hellfire, brimstone, and the devil, and kept their congregations intact by producing fear in the hearts of their little ones, telling them that if they did not do certain things and abide by the rules and regulations of the church, they would burn forever in hell.

Student: That's kind of the way I was raised.

Ramtha: My lady, you were raised in an atrocity. Did you ever wonder what happened to all those who existed before the Bible did?

Student: No. I just thought maybe hell destroyed them. Oh, well. I'm so sorry.

Ramtha: Don't be at all. That is the product of the belief.

Now here you are, an old woman. You are not youthful and zestful anymore, and you are worried about dying. And all the ominous teachings that have been programmed into you for centuries are coming to bear upon you: "Is there hell? Will I go there? Have I been so wrong?"

I tell you, you will not go to hell, for there is no such place to go. You will live in a twinkling of a moment when you pass from your body. You will be above it, and you will be a pure light entity once again. Then great teachers will come and take you to a place of further learning where you may see for yourself that what I am telling you are great truths.

Now Yeshua ben Joseph, whom you call Jesus of Nazareth, is a great God, just as you are a great God. But he is not the only son of God; he is a son of God. He was a man who became God, just as you will become God.

Student: Do you believe Jesus was a son of God?

Ramtha: I do not believe it. I know it. Just as you are a son of God.

Student: But I haven't been taught that.

Ramtha: Now, lady, what did Yeshua teach? That he is the son of God, and indeed he is. But he also openly proclaimed that everyone is also a son of God. He taught nothing other than that. Everyone is God expressing his perfection as man. And what good would it be for the Father to have so many children who are imbeciles and only one who is perfect? It would not be a very good reflection on the Father's seed.

Yeshua is your brother, not your savior. He was a man who had God within him, just as you have God within you.

Now I wish you to understand this. Yeshua lived on this plane at a time when man did not love man, when man was in bondage to man, and love was not held in high regard. But Yeshua exemplified love for everyone. It was that same love that would foster his being hailed savior of the world, for he brought love to this plane where very few expressed it and he gave it openly to everyone. He also brought the teaching that the Father is not a God of judgment and retribution but an all-loving God of mercy, grace, and compassion. Unfortunately, that understanding has been greatly altered throughout history and through the writings of those who very much failed to understand the simple teaching of this immaculate soul.

Yeshua loved. That was his great and magnificent gift to mankind. And he openly proclaimed that the source of that love was the Father that lived within him, the same Father that lived within all people. What gave Yeshua the freedom and power to embrace all humanity was that he knew that the Father and he were one and the same. He peeled away all the illusions that caused him to live an hypocrisy and, by doing so, he expressed completely the Father that lived within him. In that, Yeshua became a Christ: man expressing wholly as God; God expressing completely in man. That is what the term Christ means: God/man, man/God. A Christ is anyone who realizes that he is God and then lives that truth.

The only difference between Yeshua and you, beloved woman, is that Yeshua understood the principle of God within man and then he lived that principle completely. For that, he is indeed a grand entity. But you are also a grand entity who possesses the same nobleness and the same love to become what he became.

Yeshua is not responsible for saving you or anyone else. Through the realization that he was God living on earth, he became the savior of himself, who then taught others how to be their own salvation through the God within themselves. He taught everyone, "What I have done, all may do, for the Father and you are one. Your kingdom is not of this place. The kingdom of heaven is within you." And he spoke not of hell; he spoke of life and its beauty.

Beloved woman, love the beautiful entity that you are and the God that you are and cease reading your insidious book. Know that the Father lives within you and that you will live forever, for you will. That is simply the way it is. And besides, what would the devil do with you once he had you?

Student: I don't want to find out, but thank you.

Ramtha: My lady, what kind of Father would create such an entity and such a place and such fear and make you so helpless against all of them? He is not the God of my being nor do I acknowledge him. I acknowledge life, the Isness of all that is.

God is everything, for if there is one thing that is not God, you must ask yourself who created that. Everything is the Father, for everything is life. And the Father knows only love. He has never judged you or anyone else — ever. He has no ability to alter himself to become less than love or life.

Student: Well, God is love. I knew that.

Ramtha: And is he hate?

Student: No, I don't think he is.

Ramtha: Who is hate?

Student: I guess that's a bad one, if there is one.

Ramtha: There isn't one.

Student: Well, how are we punished then?

Ramtha: What need is there for punishment, lady? You have been doing it to yourself all of your life. Believing that you are wrong and that you are going to be punished has caused you to live in your own hell, and you have created that yourself.

There is no jailer in God's kingdom. There is no lynch-man in his kingdom. There is no tormentor. If God is love, then he is explicitly that and nothing less.

Student: After you have been taught for so long that there is a devil, how can you feel that there isn't one?

Ramtha: You know how? By knowing there isn't, by the

same process that taught you there was.

My beautiful entity, I love you greatly. Contemplate what I have told you. Love yourself and meet the Father within you. And be at peace with yourself, my lady, for when you leave this plane you are going to brightly live again.

Student: Amen.

Ramtha: So be it.

***

CHAPTER 5

Behold God

You want to see what God looks like? Go and look in a reflector. You are looking him straight in the face.

For ages you have been taught that God is outside of your kingdom, somewhere in the fathoms of space. Many of you have believed this and accepted it as a truth. But God, the principal cause of all life, has never been outside of you. It is you. It is the wonderful thought processes, the supreme intelligence that lies silent and ever-present within man.

You have been taught that you are born only to live in a moment of time, to grow old, and then die. Because you have believed that to be true, it has indeed become the reality of your life upon this plane. But I am here to help you realize that you are indeed an ongoing, immortal essence who has been living billions of years ever since God, your beloved Father, the totality of thought, contemplated itself into the brilliance of light, which each of you became. That is when each of you came to be unique and sovereign and a forever part of the mind of God.

You have been taught that God is a singular entity who with his hands made heaven and earth and then created the living creature called man. But it is you, the possessors of divine intelligence and the freedom of will, who are the great creators of all life. It is you who created the morning sun, the evening sky, and the loveliness of all things that are. It is you indeed who created the remarkable creature called man so that you, who were brilliant lights in the Void of space, could experience all the wonderment of your created forms.

My beloved brothers, the understanding of who each of you are is indeed a collection of illusions you have been living for thousands of years. You are more than merely human. You are far, far greater than the limited creature called man. You are God. You always have been; you always will be. You are the great immortal creators who have been living here life after life after life to realize this grand understanding that you allowed to be taken away from you.

All of you are God himself, created of himself. You are Gods created of God, the first and only direct creation of the source of all life. In your adventures into the exploration of life, you have integrated your supreme intelligence with cellular matter to become God/man — the mind of God expressing in the form called humanity — Gods living in the wonderment of their own creation, termed man. Mankind, womankind, humanity: It is God indeed wonderfully disguised as limited, wretched entities.

Who are you? Why are you here? What is your purpose and your destiny? Do you think you are merely a creature of coincidence born to live in a wisp of time and then to be no more, indeed? What makes you think you did not live before? Why now? And why you?

You have lived upon this plane thousands of lifetimes, and you have come and gone like a fickle wind. You have lived every face, every color, every creed, every religion. You have warred and been warred upon. You have been king and servant alike. You have been sailor and captain. You have been conqueror and conquered. You have been everything there is in all of your historical understandings. Why? For the purpose of feeling, for the purpose of wisdom, for the purpose of identifying the greatest mystery of all times — you.

Where do you think you came from? Do you think you are simply a wretched bunch of cellular mass that has evolved from a singular cell? Then who is it that peers so intently from behind your eyes? What is the essence that gives you your uniqueness and personality, your character and zest, your ability to love, to embrace, to hope, to dream, and the awesome power to create? And where did you accumulate all the intelligence, all the knowledge, all the wisdom that you display, even as a little child? Do you think you became what you are merely in one lifetime that is only a breath in eternity?

Everything that you are, you have become over the vastness of time by living life after life after life. And from each of those life experiences, you have gathered to you the wisdom that has helped to formulate the uniqueness and the beauty called you. You are much too priceless; you are much too beautiful to have been created for only a moment's siege upon the eternalness of time.

You think your parents created you? Your mother and father are your genetic parents but they did not create you. In a greater understanding, they are your beloved brothers. And you are indeed as old as they are, for all entities were created in the same moment. All were born when God, the grand and magnificent thought, contemplated and expanded itself into the brilliance of light. That is when you came to be; that is when you were born. Your true parent is God, the Mother/Father Principle of all life.

You think your body is you? 'Tis not. Your body is only a cloak that represents the unseen essence that is your true identity: the collection of feeling attitudes, called your personality self, that lies within your embodiment.

Ponder this for a moment: What do you love about another entity? Is it the body? No. It is the essence of another that you love, the unseen personality self that lies behind the eyes. What you love about another is the unseen essence that makes the body work, that makes the eyes flicker, the voice melodious, the hair have sheen, the hands have touch.

Your body is indeed a wonderful, refined machine, as it were, but it is nothing without that which works it, which is you. What you are is not your embodiment but a collection of thoughts or feeling attitudes, which presents itself as a unique personality self. And have you ever seen your thoughts? Have you ever seen your personality? What about your laughter? Can you hear it without your body? You have not the conception of how grand you really are, for what you truly are is as unseen as the wind. As I am an enigma to you, so are you to yourself the greatest enigma of all.

Do you know what you are without your pretenses, without the masks that you wear, without your armor of hard-heartedness? Within the core of your being you are indeed God. God, the great mystery to mankind, has never been outside of you, for what lies behind your eyes — beneath your fine linen, beyond the illusion of your face — is the unseen virtue of thought called God, the personality self that makes you you. The God within you is the sublime intelligence that gives you credence and the awesome power to create. It is the wonderful life force that maintains your life forever and ever and ever.

The body that you inhabit is a magnificent creation of Gods: you and your beloved brothers. It was created so that you, an unseen essence of thought and emotion, could interact with the life you created upon this plane. The creature called man was created simply as a vehicle to express through so that through the senses of the embodiment all of the creations upon this plane could be experienced and understood by the Gods who created them in the beginning.

The body was created to house a most complex electrical system of light variables that make up and constitute the true entity self. What you really are is not the size of your body. You are a little pinpoint of light. In the smallness of your being is collected everything that you have ever been since you were born of God, your beloved Father.

You, the God principle, are not a flesh entity. You are a rounded, fiery, pure-energy, light principle living within a body to obtain the prize of creative life called emotion. What you truly are is not what you inhabit; it is what you feel. You are known by your emotions, not by your body.

What you truly are is Spirit and soul, a light entity and an emotional entity combined. Your Spirit — this little point of light — surrounds all molecular structures of your body; thus it houses and supports the mass of your embodiment. Your soul lies within the mass, near your heart, in a cavity under a shield of bone wherein nothing exists except electrical energy. Your soul records and stores, in the form of emotion, every thought you have ever entertained. It is because of the unique collectiveness of emotion stored within your soul that you have a unique ego identity or personality self. The body that you inhabit is simply a carriage — a chosen, refined vehicle — that allows you to live and play upon a plane of matter. Yet through your vehicle you have steeped yourself in the illusion that your body is who you are. 'Tis not. Just as God is imageless, so be you.

Great creative God that you are, who do you think has created your life? Do you believe that a supreme being or forces outside of you have controlled your life? That is not the truth as it is known. All you have ever done, been, or experienced, you are wholly responsible for. You, who have the power to create the magnificence of stars, have created every moment and every circumstance of your life. Who you are, you chose to be. What you look like, you created. How you live, you wholly designed and destined. That is the exercise and privilege, if you will, of being God/man.

You create your life through your own thought processes by how you think. Everything you think, you will feel; and all that you feel manifests to create the conditions of your life.

Ponder this: It only takes you a moment to envision happiness, and your whole body will feel joyful. It only takes you a moment to play the part of a wretched creature whom no one has befriended, and you will feel sorrow and pity for yourself. It only takes a moment to do that. It takes you but a moment to stop weeping and to laugh with glee. It takes you a moment to stop judging and feel the beauty of all things. Now who is doing all of this? You. And while you have had this fancy of creating feelings within your being, has anything around you changed? No. But everything that you are, has.

You are precisely what you are thinking. Everything you think, so will it be in your life. If you ponder a fantasy of copulation, your being will become enticed. If you ponder misery, you will have misery. If you ponder unhappiness, you will have it. If you ponder joy, you will have it. If you ponder genius, it is already there.

How is your future created? Through thought. All of your tomorrows are designed by your thoughts this very day, for every thought you entertain — every fantasy you have, for whatever emotional purpose — creates a feeling within your body, which is recorded within your soul. That feeling then sets a precedent for the conditions in your life, for it will draw to you circumstances that will create and match the same feeling that has been recorded in your soul. And know that every word you utter is creating your days to come, for words are only sounds that express the feelings within your soul that have been given birth through thought.

Do you think that things happen to you simply by chance? That is not the truth as it is known. There is no such thing as an accident or a coincidence in this kingdom. And no one is a victim of anyone else's will or designs. Everything that happens to you, you have thought and felt into your life. Either it has been fantasized in what-ifs or in fears, or someone has told you that something would be and you accepted it as a truth. Everything that happens, happens as an intentional act that is ordained through thought and emotion. Everything.

Everything you have ever thought — every fantasy you have ever had, all the things you have spoken — have all come to pass or are waiting to come to pass. For how think you everything is created? It is created through thought. Thought is the true giver of life that never dies, that never can be destroyed, and you have used it to think yourself into life, for it is your link to the mind of God.

For ages entities have tried to teach you this truth through riddles, through songs, through writings, but most of you have refused to realize it because few have wanted to have the responsibility for their lives on their own shoulders. But the way this kingdom works is that everything you think — every attitude you hold toward yourself, the Father, life — will become, from the vilest and ugliest of things to the most exquisite and supreme of things, for only you know the difference. The Father knows only life. So you get what you speak. You are what you think. You "am" what you conclude.

The less you think of yourself, the less you become. The less you give credit to yourself for having intelligence, the more of an imbecile you become. The less beautiful you think you are, the more ugly you become. The more impoverished you think you are, the more wretched you become because you have ordained it to be so.

Contemplate how great the love of God is, that it allows you to be and to create for yourself anything you wish, yet never judges you. Contemplate the love that it has for you, such that it manifests for you every thought you embrace and every word you utter. Contemplate it.

So who is the creator of your life? You. Who is the designer of your life? You. All that you are and all that you have experienced, you have created through your own collective reasoning through thought, which is God. You have accepted into your life precisely all that you have desired to accept, and you have experienced life according to your accepted values. It is you who determine what is good for you, what is to be accepted by you, what is to be experienced by you. It is you, by your own thinking.

You are not a slave or servant or puppet of some deity that watches you in your struggles. You live in the awesomeness of life in exquisite freedom. Each of you has the freedom of will to accept and embrace whatever thoughts you choose and, with that awesome power, you have created everything for yourself. Your every thought creates the destiny that lies before you. Your every feeling creates your path called life. Whatever you think and then feel, so will it be in your life, for the Father says, "Every emotion, so be it."

Who are you? You are God who possesses within the silence of your being the ability to think, the ability to create, and the ability to become whatever you want to become, for you are this moment precisely what you chose to be, and none has stayed your hand in becoming it. You are the lawgiver, the supreme creator of your life and life circumstances. You are indeed the supreme ruler of an all-wise intelligence that you have failed to fully realize in this and many other lives.

Once you could create a flower. But what do you create for yourselves now? Your greatest creations are unhappiness, worry, pity, misery, hatred, dissension, self-denial, age, disease, and death. You create for yourselves a life of limitation by accepting limiting beliefs, which then become steadfast truths within your beings and thus the reality of your lives. You separate yourselves from life by judging all things, all people, and even yourselves. You live by a code of fashion called beauty and surround yourselves with things that permit you to be accepted by the limited consciousness of man, which accepts nothing but its own unattainable ideal. You are babes who are born to grow up, lose the vitality in your bodies, and believe yourselves into old age until you perish.

You, the great creative Gods who were once the winds of freedom, have become herdlike entities who cloister in great cities and live in fear behind locked doors. Instead of towering mountains and wonderful winds, you have great buildings and a terrifying consciousness. You have created a society that regulates how you should think, what you should believe, how you should act, and what you should look like.

You fear war and the rumors of war. You fear diseasements. You fear unacknowledgment. You tremble to look into the eyes of another, yet you hunger for the affection called love. You question every good thing that happens to you and doubt if it will ever happen again. You grovel in the marketplace for success and fame, for gold and rupees and drachmas and dollars and, ah, but for a bit of joy.

You have thought yourselves into despair. You have thought yourselves into unworthiness. You have thought yourselves into failure. You have thought yourselves into disease. You have thought yourselves into death. All of those things you have created, for the fiery creator within — who has the power to take a thought and create universes or set stars ablaze in the heavens for an eternity — has entrapped itself into belief and dogma, fashion and tradition, limited thought by limited thought by limited thought. And it is your own disbeliefs that have not allowed you to live.

What do you disbelieve in? Everything that you cannot perceive through your bodily senses; anything that cannot be heard, seen, touched, tasted, or smelled. Yet show me a belief; put it in my hand. Show me an emotion; I want to touch it. Show me a thought; where is it? Show me your attitude; what does it look like? Show me the image of the wind. And show me time, that has taken away the precious moments of your life.

You have disbelieved in the greatest gifts of life and, because of that, you have not allowed a more unlimited understanding to occur. Life upon life, existence upon existence, you became so immersed in the illusions of this plane that you forgot the wonderful fire that flows through you. In ten and one-half million years you have come from being sovereign and all-powerful entities to where you are utterly lost in matter; enslaved by your own creations of dogma, law, fashion, and tradition; separated by country, creed, sex, and race; immersed in jealousy, bitterness, guilt, and fear. You so identified yourselves with your bodies that you entrapped yourselves in survival and forgot the unseen essence that you truly are, the God within you that allows you to create your dreams however you choose. Immortality you have openly rejected, and for that you will die and return here again and again and again. Thus here you are again after ten and one-half million years of living here, and yet you hold onto your disbeliefs.

God, the totality of thought, is a grand stage indeed. And he allows you to write your own script and play it, part by part, upon the stage. And when your curtains are drawn, the last word is spoken and the last bow is taken, you die. For what reason? Because you, supreme lawmaker, believe you will.

This life is all a game. It is an illusion. All of it is. But you, the players, have come to believe that it is the only reality. Yet the only reality that has ever existed and ever will exist is life, a free, ongoing essence of being that allows you to create your games however you wish to play them.

When you realize that you have the power to think yourself into ignorance, disease, and death, you will also realize that you have the power to become grander simply by opening yourself up to a more unlimited thought flow, which allows you to have greater genius, greater creativity, and life forever. When you realize that the God who created the body in the first place is the power that sits within you, then your body will never age or become diseased, nor will it ever perish. But as long as you hold onto your beliefs and limit your thinking, you will never experience the unlimitedness which gave glory to the morning sun and mystery to the evening sky.

What happens when you have decreed yourself to perish from this place? Well, the body dies but you who think, in the silentness behind your eyes, always live. When you leave this plane, if you choose to die, the true you will not be buried into the ground and go to the worm and then to ash. You are ongoing with the wind. Where you go is where you came from, and there you decide what you wish to do upon your next adventure, for that is what this all is. And you shall return here however many times you desire to return until you reclaim your identity as God. Then you are off on a grander adventure indeed, in another heaven, in another place.

You are loved greater than you have ever imagined, for no matter what you do, you will still live. So why have you worried? Why have you fought? Why have you diseased yourself? Why have you sorrowed yourself? Why have you limited yourself? Why have you not enjoyed the splendor of the sunrise, the freedom of the wind, and the laughter of a child? Why have you not lived instead of struggling?

You are going to live again and again. Your seed is perpetual; it is forever. Despite all your disbeliefs — no matter how greatly you limit your kingdom, no matter how much you worry and despair — there is one thing you will never do away with, and that is called life. No matter how blind and unaccepting you are, you will always have life, for that is the value called God, and that is you.

This life you are living is a dream — a great dream — a

façade, if you will. It is thought playing with matter, and it creates deep realities that bind your emotions to this plane until you, the dreamer, wake up.

You never knew how beautiful you were, for you never really looked at yourself. You never looked at who you are and what you are. You want to see what God looks like? Go and look in a reflector. You are looking him straight in the face.

Know that you have worth. There is no value to assess your worth. And there is no image to portray your beauty. And there is no end to your kingdom.

The greatest sermon ever delivered was by a great master upon a mountaintop. As he stood there looking upon the masses who came to listen to him, he said unto them, "Behold God." That was all he ever needed to say — behold God — for each had created his limitations, his desires and diseasements, his wealth or his poverty, his joy and his sorrow, his life and his death.

Behold God. Remember that, for you are he that lives in everything. One day you will behold God. Touch the Self; that is all you need to do.

***

CHAPTER 6

Life After Life

Death is a great illusion, for what is created can never be destroyed. Death is of the body only. The personality self that lives within the walls of flesh is ongoing.

Are you any less than the blossoms? What is their life? They are born of pregnant buds that burst into full bloom from the warming rays of the sun. Their wonderful essence fills the air with an aroma that causes all things to rejoice in the promise of new life. They enhance the birds in their flight, the bees in their labors, and man in his delight and quest for love.

So the wonderful flower sets a seed so that it might come again. And when the bloom falls off and the fruit comes forth, ah, that is termed wisdom. That is the product of life. And when the fruit is consumed and the spice and harvest of autumn are upon the land, the tree begins to shiver with a northerly wind, begins to lose its wonderful leaves until it stands there, blatantly bare.

When the great white silence comes and fills the boughs of the trees with a thickening, glistening brilliance and all is cold and barren, where be the blossom? It is in the memory. It is in the wisdom. It is in the growth of last spring and it is coming forth again, for when the season has turned and winter is gone, the buds come again and, behold, there is another blossom.

If the ongoingness of life is beheld in a single blossom, why do you think that you are any less than its life? Do you think that you only bloom in spring, produce your fruit in summer, drop your leaves in autumn, and then die in winter? But are you not greater than the greatest blossom? Is not your life more important? Indeed it is. And as the blossoms continue to bloom every spring, so will you live life after life after life.

What a story your blossoms could tell of all the seasons you have seen.

Student: My mother died last year and I want to know if she is still alive and, if she is, is she happy.

Ramtha: Do you believe in death, master?

Student: Sometimes I do. But most of the time I have this feeling that perhaps we still live. I have three children, and what I've noticed about them, even from the time they were just born, is that each one had a very distinct personality, which really hasn't changed very much as they have become older. Even our cats and dogs had a very definite personality from the time they were very little. Sometimes I just can't believe that their personalities develop only in this life. So it makes me think that possibly we've lived before and continue to live.

Ramtha: Very wise observation, entity. I will tell you a great truth, and I wish for you never to forget this: Life never ends. It is true that you can mutilate the body — you can hack its head off, disembowel it, and do every wretched thing you can to it — but you can never destroy the personality self that lives within the embodiment. Contemplate for a moment how one could destroy, blow up, knife, or war against a thought. You cannot. And the life force of all inhabited creatures, human or animal, is the unseen collective of thought and emotion called the personality self that lives behind the mask of the body.

What gives virtue, vitality, and character to the embodiment is the unseen virtue of thought, which is energy. That is what makes the mouth work, the eyes work, the limbs work, this wondrous energy that is pulling all the little strings, as it were. Nothing can ever destroy energy. Nothing can take the life force from any one thing.

Death is a great illusion, for what has been created can never be destroyed. Death is of the body only. The essence that inhabits and operates the body will soon come back and integrate with another embodiment, if it wishes to, for the life force that lives within the walls of flesh is ongoing. Remember that.

Now let me tell you what happens to entities who pass from this plane. When the body can no longer be effective, the energy — the soul — is withdrawn by the Spirit of the entity. Everything has a soul. Even animals possess a Spirit and a soul. If they didn't, they would not possess the energy and creativity necessary to sustain their life.

Once the Spirit calls forth the soul and loosens it from its cavity, things become tranquil and peaceful. There is a saying associated with your religion: "Behold, in the cradle of God there is no more pain, no more tears, and no more sorrow." That is a truth because when you pass from this plane, you are freed from the instincts and sensations of the body. That means you no longer experience fear, or the aches and pains of the body, or the hunger of the body, or the illusion of time that causes anxiety. All things associated with the physical body are no longer, and you are in what is called utopia. You are in the cradle of God.

The death of the body is like going into slumber. Once the Spirit calls forth the soul, it travels up through the energy centers in the body called seals or chakras. The soul, which is memory, leaves the cellular mass of the body through the last of the seals, the seventh seal — called the pituitary gland — which is located in the center of the head. That passage is often experienced as traveling through a tunnel, accompanied by the sound of wind. The light that is seen at the end of the tunnel is the light of your being, the Spirit of your being. Once the soul leaves the body, the body expires and the entity becomes a free soul-self. It takes but a moment and it is painless.

At the moment of death, things begin to illuminate and become awesomely bright, for the moment you pass this plane, you go out of the density of matter and back into a light existence. There you are simply powerful mind and emotion, and your body is a body of light, changing in its electrical form according to the thoughts that are accepted through your light form. From that point you go to one of seven heavens. Which heaven you go to is determined by the attitudes that you emotionally expressed upon this plane.

Now what you term heaven is simply life and its different levels or planes. Yeshua ben Joseph spoke of seven heavens. Well, there are indeed seven heavens, which are actual places or planes of existence, and this plane is one of them. And in none of the planes is there any such place as hell to torment or punish mankind. He does that well enough himself. When you leave the embodiment, you always go to the heaven or vibratory level that is aligned with whatever consciousness understanding or collective emotional attitudes you expressed upon this plane.

There are seven realizations or levels-of-consciousness understanding. The seven understandings are those of reproduction and survival, fear and pain, power, felt love, expressed love, God seen in all life, and God I Am.

For you to understand: Every thought you contemplate and embrace for an understanding has a vibratory frequency, which is experienced as a feeling. Thus if you are mastering the understanding of pain, you are contemplating the more limited thoughts associated with pain, which gives rise to the lower vibratory frequencies that are emotionally experienced as pain. If you are contemplating and mastering the understanding of love and the expression of it, you will experience the elation of the higher vibratory frequencies of the thoughts of love shared and expressed. Wherever your consciousness is predominantly focused for your understanding, that is the heaven to which you will go, for the magnetic field of your aura, the Spirit of your being, will draw you to the vibration of that plane.

Now your mother has passed this plane into a state of great peace and great rest, which she very much desired and needed. She has gone to the level of heaven that she has drawn to her, according to the consciousness understanding that she has acquired. She is now in a state of her level, just as you are now here in a state of this level. Her level is a fourth level, which is aligned with the emotional attitude of love felt but not expressed. Your mother is a great feeling entity but often she could not express her feelings. You and the husband of her being often failed to understand her because she could not communicate most of her feelings.

Your mother is now in a great level, and she will stay there for as long as she wishes. When she contemplates the thought of advancement, she will then continue her expansion into the other dimensions of thought in a light-level existence, or she can return back to this plane, the first plane, into whatever genetic pattern she feels would be best to express through and continue her advancement all the way to the seventh level of understanding on this plane, the plane of density in matter.

This plane, this heaven, is called the plane of demonstration, for here is where entities can witness in matter their creative power and whatever attitudes they are expressing in emotion. This is the only plane of the seven that has darkness upon it and the only one where you cannot hear the music of light. It is a plane where entities are born of great knowingness only to undergo the programming of social consciousness into unknowingness. That is what happens here, and that is why it is often very arduous to advance upon this plane.

If your mother chooses to return here, she will have the option to become the babe of one of your children or of your children's children. If she returns in your lifetime, she will return as a babe of your daughter, when she decides to bear children. And you will know your mother, if you allow yourself to, for when you look upon the babe you will have a feeling that transcends the obvious looks and appearances. That is how you will know her.

Is your mother aware of you? Very much, for when you pass this plane, you are much more aware than when you are in an embodiment. You can tune in, as it were, to all levels of which you are aware, for you are no longer engrossed in the density of matter. You are in a lighter density, a higher vibration; thus you have the ability to see other vibratory levels which exist parallel to yours and appear as thought forms, light forms. So your mother is very much aware of you, if she chooses to be as, when you pass, you will be very aware of those who are here, if you wish to be.

Is your mother happy? If you are not happy here, your unhappiness is only amplified when you pass, for when you are without the body you are in a state of pure feeling and emotion, so your emotions are amplified and intensified. But from that amplification, you quickly learn to manifest whatever level you need in order to continue to grow in your understanding of joy.

I will tell you of one plane where if you ever look upon it you will be saddened greatly in your being. It is a plane of many entities who are expressing on the first and second levels of consciousness. It is like a plain, a place that is level. And what will you find there? You will not find mountains and rivers, grass and flora and sky in their light forms. You will find billions of entities in their light embodiments laid out in endless rows. They are lying there in slumber living the illusion that they are dead, because they steadfastly believe that life does not exist beyond the grave. Even though their thought is still alive and magnetic and compulsive and volatile, in its energy it thinks it is dead, though it is really still alive. Remember, whatever we steadfastly believe, we will convince ourselves that it is true; and whatever we know as a truth will transform itself into a reality. That is how powerful our creativity and our wills are.

Many of the entities there were taught that when they died, they would be dead until a messiah returned for them and, through fear and the feeling of being alienated from divine love, they accepted that teaching as a truth. Thus in the last moments before their deaths, they believed they would go to a place to await a resurrection. So on this level, there are rows and rows of entities waiting to be resurrected by someone whom they believe to be grander than they. Though we have tried to awaken them — and there are a few who have awakened and arisen — most were also taught that a devil of some sort would appear and try to tempt them into arising. Thus they also know that to be a truth. So no matter who tries to awaken them, they refuse to wake up. And it may take thousands of years before they realize they are alive and thus awake from their slumber. A most unfortunate teaching.

That is the only painful place there is, the plane where entities have believed such understandings into an absolute knowingness. And as far as you can see there, you have brothers who are lying in slumber. Every other plane is magnificent life.

Student: Ramtha, is it possible to see or communicate with those who have died?

Ramtha: Do you wish to see your mother?

Student: Yes, I do, very much.

Ramtha: So be it. We will see if this is agreeable with her and, if so, we will arrange a time for you to see her. But it will come when you least expect it, so you will know that you didn't just imagine it.

Now for you to know the reason you will see your mother as light is not that she is greater than you. The light is the radiant speed at which her essence vibrates; it is the speed that gives off that light. Yet you possess the same thing. When you see the light of the entity, it is simply because she is in a greater vibration interacting with a lower plane.

There is a host of entities from the fifth plane who are gathered in this very audience, for there are entities who are a part of this audience whom they love. They are the glimmering lights that you may see out of the side of your eye. If you look at them directly with the part of your eye that is predominantly made up of cones, you will not see them, yet they are here. You have learned?

Student: Yes, very much. Thank you.

Ramtha: Good. A good thing to know: Never believe in anything. Never. That is convincing yourself of something you have yet to know and understand through experience. And belief is very dangerous because, in belief, you are placing your life, your attitudes, and your trust in something which has not founded itself as a truth within your being, which causes you to become very vulnerable. And in that state of vulnerability, you can be manipulated, accursed, damned, and can lose your life, all because of belief.

Know whatever it is you wish to know, and you can do that simply by asking for the understanding and then listening to the feelings within your being. Always trust the wisdom of your feelings. Never go against them and try to force a belief upon yourself that doesn't feel good inside.

Another thing: Learn to have compassion for murderers

and slayers, for they have a terrible working through of emotion that they must deal with when their conquest is finished, and that often takes millenniums. The slain has a body within the next moment. The slayer never forgets.

Student: When one passes from this earthly life, where does he go in order to assess his life and decide what he will do in his next life?

Ramtha: To the plane or heaven that is aligned with the collective attitudes that he is in the process of understanding.

For example, you, entity, have mastered the understandings of what is termed survival in limitation all the way through pain, power, love unspoken, and are expressing on the fifth plane of consciousness, which is realized love, spoken love, expressed love. If you were to pass this plane at this time, you would go to the fifth plane of heaven called paradise, for that is the greatest understanding of which you could be aware.

In other words, master, what you have come to know and understand is far-encompassing, for you are beginning to understand and realize your own worth and value, the preciousness of yourself, the sovereignty of your truth, and the power of your own thought processes. You are beginning to see the beauty of yourself in the life around you, and you are growing in your compassion for others and in your respect for the preciousness of all life. You are expressing all of these truths because from experience and your contemplative thought processes, you have come to embrace these as ideals of being, as truths to be realized within the kingdom of self. And that speaks well of how far you have come in your consciousness understanding. Yet there are greater understandings, more unlimited states of being still to be seen, experienced, and understood. But you cannot begin to entertain these understandings or embrace them as ideals until you first come to know and understand what you are now expressing, for wisdom builds upon itself to encompass greater and greater understanding.

For example, you cannot truly see or be aware of the beauty of all life or express the depths of love and compassion for others until you have first seen your own sublime beauty and expressed love and compassion for yourself. Once love of self has become real in an understanding, then you have a basis from which to expand your understanding to embrace life outside of you. And once that understanding is realized and known, you will begin to realize that you are the life that you perceive to be outside you. You see?

So if you passed from this plane, you would go to a plane of consciousness understanding aligned with your thought processes and expressive emotional attitudes. You could not go to a plane of a more unlimited understanding because you have yet to perceive that such an understanding exists, for it has not become the reality of self.

Student: So our life will always be exactly whatever our thoughts are, whether on this plane or the plane that we go to when we leave here.

Ramtha: That is correct. That is why I am teaching you how to become more unlimited in your thought processes, for the more unlimited your thinking becomes, the more unlimited your life shall become, wherever you are. The greater the heaven you create here within your own kingdom of thought and emotion, the greater the heaven you will experience when you leave this plane or, if you choose, when you return here. Those whose thoughts are steeped in guilt, judgment of self and others, and bitterness and hatred toward their brothers will leave this plane only to continue to experience those attitudes until they learn from them, until they have had their gut full of them and realize that there are grander ways to be and greater heavens to experience.

Student: You say there are seven planes. Could you describe what the other planes are, especially the seventh.

Ramtha: This plane that you are upon is the first plane, the plane of three-dimensional perception. This is the plane where entities gain the understanding of God in the form called matter. And it is a great mastery to live here, for you must enter this plane through the birth processes and survive the limitations and instincts of flesh.

Upon this plane, all levels of consciousness understanding

exist, for this is the plane of what is termed expressive God or the plane of demonstration. It is the plane where you can demonstrate and witness consciousness in the material form in order to expand your emotional understanding. And I wish you to know that this place of yours called Earth is only one of innumerable places where an entity can experience and express through an embodiment upon the plane of demonstration.

The second plane is the plane of those who are experiencing for their understanding pain, remorse, and guilt. The plane of the third is called the plane of power. That is the plane where one seeks to control and enslave others not through copulation or physical means — for they do not have that — but through what is termed mind thoughts, trying to get all to see their point of view. The fourth is the plane of love. All on this plane love deeply but, unfortunately, they cannot express that deepness. Thus they are living a light-level existence in which they are experiencing great love but without the ability to express that love.

The fifth plane is called paradise. It is the first plane that has the enrapturement of what is called the golden light. Imagine a light that is like the light from your sun but it is golden. On the fifth plane, that color envelops all things and yet all things retain the vividness of their unique colors. And there, there is no night, only the golden light. And music — wondrous music — is heard, for the light that envelops all things vibrates at the tone of its color in a wondrous harmonic movement. This harmonic movement is the breath of life there, not air. Thus on the plane of paradise, one breathes sound and music and lives in light.

You know, on your plane, the first plane, there are those who have understood and mastered copulation, pain, and power, and they have brought love into an expressed reality. And they have accomplished it rather easily here. Mastery of the sixth and seventh levels of understanding is not as easily accomplished on the plane of demonstration because those understandings are beyond demonstration. But those who live on the first plane and who love — who express their love outwardly through words and deeds and actions, and desire for their life to be lived through love — when they pass from this plane, they go to the fifth. And on the plane of paradise, there are entities who are billions of years old who have found paradise to be such a wonderful place that they do not realize there is yet more to come.

On the fifth plane you have the power to express and manifest your love. And whatsoever you desire in the moment, so it will come to pass. If a fisherman, a lover of fish, is desirous to have fish, he will go to a lake that will be before him. The lake will be surrounded with tall cypresses, poplars, and whatever else he loves. If he loves the lake as it appears in autumn, the poplars will become the color of cinnamon and the cypresses will remain in the depths of their emeraldness. And when he sits down to cast his line for fish, if he desires a cool breeze, there will come a cool breeze blowing gently across the lake. And when the entity casts a feeble and humble worm into the center of the wondrous lake and imagines what he desires to catch, behold, he will catch it. Then he takes the fish — which are like the fish on this plane — back to the home of his dreams and he consumes them, for that makes him happy, for he loves what he has done.

Entities there cannot imagine a place being greater than that one. That is why it is called paradise. And it is a difficult plane to achieve for those who have not realized and expressed love.

Once one has expressed upon the fifth plane for a while, he will eventually question the essence of the light that envelops all things and why he has deserved to be there. Many do not question why they deserve to be in paradise; they merely accept it. But eventually he will ponder whence come the light and the music. Then he will begin to see a splendid life force energy that has an equalness, an equality with the light, with the flora, with the fishes, with the lake, with the poplars in their cinnamon color of autumn. And he will begin to contemplate the equalness of all these things. When he has done so, he will begin to see that no thing is separate, that all things are in a flow of oneness. When he begins to see that — when he takes all the love that has been understood and realized through the expression of it and begins to contemplate the oneness of all things, all entities — then he will advance to the sixth plane of understanding.

The sixth plane of heaven is beyond words, for words cannot describe how you — who believe yourself to be separate from the plant and the wind and the one who sits next to you — can be completely at one with something, yet unique and separate from that which you are at one with. But the plane of the sixth is the door to the seventh, for whatever one perceives and knows to be a reality, he will always become completely. So when one sees only God in a oneness and lives in that sphere of oneness, he will become that which he sees and lives with. And the superlativeness and supremeness of that becoming are the seventh heaven. The door to that heaven is the sixth plane of understanding, which is seeing what you become: pure God, pure reason, pure thought, pure life, pure light, the substance and basis of the totality of all that is.

Now the seventh: Imagine a brilliance that is greater than brilliance, and the evolving core of the brilliance is of a hue of such color that the color no longer has brilliance but is in a state of emitting brilliance. In the core of that brilliance there are flashes of such wonderment. And the sea that the core is in is moving and expanding and rolling upward. And as the core rolls upward, the brilliance of the core emits a spectacular light review. And as the light review goes off into the perimeters of the brilliance, the core continues to evolve, to be.

That which reaches out of the core is you. That which is called you — who reaches out of the core to add to the spectacularness of the brilliance — is one who has contemplated the thought of the core and has become it in a unique form ongoing.

You who have contemplated the core and become it have now become the platform from which all life springs forth, for what comes forth from the emission of the core into brilliance is thought. And from the thought that you have become in an ongoing, unique form, you will feed and nurture and expand the consciousness of all life.

Very poor be my words, for the vision must go beyond the bounds of space, time, and measure — beyond the limitation of speech — into an emotional understanding. But I assure you, master, as you evolve and expand your understanding — moment to moment, step by step, realization upon realization — your vista will become evermore expansive until your emotion encompasses all that is. And that is when you will be joy. That is the seventh plane. That is God. That is where all in the eventuality will come to be.

Student: I would like to know why people come back to this plane.

Ramtha: There are as many reasons, master, as there are entities upon this plane. But most entities keep coming back to this plane because they have lived many lives here and this is familiar to them; this is home to them. It is their roots, as it were. And when they leave here, they leave behind many entities with whom they have great emotional attachments, which may arise from guilt or hate, as well as love. So when they pass this plane, their attachment to this place and to other entities creates an emotional tie that draws them back here life after life after life.

Then there are those adventurers who go to many other places to experience there and then bring their understanding and experiences back to this plane. And there are yet others who are complete with the experiences of this plane and never again return here but go on to other places.

Student: You have said that once a person dies, he goes to one of several places or heavens, as you call them, depending upon what his attitudes are like, and there he decides whether he wants to come back here.

Ramtha: That is indeed correct.

Student: How is that decision made? Who makes that decision? Does each individual decide that for himself?

Ramtha: There is no one who sits aloft, master, and governs or directs any one entity to choose a particular plane or place for expression, regardless of how the entity expressed in a prior life.

To answer your question, let me tell you of an entity who lived upon your plane many years ago in your time. When the entity passed from this plane, he had experienced and understood power and pain, and he had expressed the sweetness and tenderness of love. That means his understanding was aligned with the fifth plane of heaven. Thus when he left this plane, that is where he went for what is termed a holiday of whatever duration he desired.

Now the fifth plane is a plane where entities readily manifest through their thoughts — which is their voice — whatever they imagine, whatever they desire, and in but a moment it appears. They experience color and form and illusion and all things in life. And they continue to experience all of their dreams for however long they desire, until the time comes when they ponder whether there is something more. And there is something more, for there are still two heavens beyond them that they cannot see, for they have not reckoned with those understandings in their thought processes nor expressed them in their lives. To experience those planes, they have to see God in all things and be as God is. Though they have humbly expressed love, they have yet to understand their oneness with God and all life.

After a short time upon the plane of paradise, this master began to ponder whether there was something more, and he called for help. And there is always help. Behold, there appeared before him a most wondrous entity, silken in light and arrayed in garments that are brilliant to the eye. And he said to the entity, "O master, I am troubled. In this paradise I have everything. I have the fishes from the sea that I always dreamed about catching and never did. I have the home I always dreamed about having and never did. And I have flowers that do not even need a gardener. A most wondrous place. And look at my garments. I never had clothes like this before, but I have them now. Yet I am still troubled. Though I have many friends here, the woman I love is not with me. And that is not all that troubles me. Where is God? I see all these wondrous things. I have all these wondrous things. But where is God?"

The wise entity says unto him, "Blessed be you who have reveled in all things that are and yet question whether there is perhaps something more, who questions where the Father is who has adorned you so well."

"Well, that is what I am mostly troubled about. I would

like to thank God for giving me all of these wonderful things. Although I've always been a little afraid of God, I would like to pay homage to him, if that's acceptable."

The entity says, "Master, come with me. There is a place I wish to take you to."

In but a blink of the eye, they are at a pond, yet they have traveled nowhere. The wise entity says, "Master, do sit yourself beside me and look into the water."

The man looks into the water, and what does he see? He sees before him his last expression upon this plane: from the time he was a babe suckling upon his mother's breast, to the changing of his sweet bottom, to youth and skinned knees and lost marbles, to young manhood and seducing some unwilling participant, to manhood, marriage, and love forever, to children and opportunities, labors and friends and finances.

He is amazed, for he is seeing himself as he has never seen himself before. He had been a good man in that life, who believed that God existed. He had been a powerful man, and yet he never enslaved anyone with his power. And he had loved his wife and children earnestly and didn't mind telling a few about that either. So he had made himself known in that life by teaching and mastering and loving and becoming humble and pure in Spirit.

As his life is revealed in the pond and he contemplates what he sees, the man looks at the entity and he says, "I have done well."

The entity says, "You have done well. You have done very well indeed, save for this: You never sought to know who your Father is, and you always separated him from yourself and all life.

"Your wife, let us look at her. The greatest part of your love for your wife was giving her the things that she adored so much. And in that regard you've done quite well, save for this: You never loved yourself enough to allow her to love you in spite of all the things you gave her. You never really appreciated how grand you truly are, the giver of all those things.

"So to ease your troubles, let me suggest this to you: Go back. It is there that you have expressed, and it is there that you have gained. And this time, you will have for yourself the mastery of loving yourself, expressing the love within your being, and seeing God in the beauty of all things.

"If you decide to return, let me suggest that you choose carefully who you shall be, so the role that is laid out before you will give you the opportunity to become who you are and to understand what you have yet to understand.

"I will leave you alone for a while. Ponder these things. You may take all the time you need. And if you decide to return, let me know and I will show you how best to proceed."

The man is sitting there, a little weary, and he ponders. He has everything that he never had before; if he goes back, he loses it. Yet he is troubled, for he is desirous to find this God who has blessed him with paradise. So he calls for the entity and says unto him, "Entity, I am desirous to see God. But I'm not sure how I am supposed to do this."

The entity says, "All you need do, master, is decide when you would like to present yourself known. Any time period, any place would be appropriate, because what you are going to set into motion by your desires will provide the experiences you are needing, regardless of when or where you choose. But if you have a particular desire to be a part of your family again, I would suggest to you — and it is only a suggestion — that you stay with them, for with them you have accomplished the most learning to this point."

The man ponders this for a moment and then he says, "O entity, I have one further question to ask you: How will I know this God when I see him?" The entity replies to him, "When you know yourself, you will know him."

This lightens the man's heart greatly. For the first time in his existence he can relate to a God that is perhaps the same as he. So he says to the entity, "I am desirous to go back and to see God. And I wish to be part of my family again."

The entity says to him, "Look into the pool. What do you see?" The man looks into the pool and, behold, the young son that he left is now a young man who has escorted and wooed some lovely enchantress. They have become enamored with one another, and the copulation processes have already begun.

The entity says, "There is a good chance, master, that there is a way provided for you to return through the offspring of your son."

"Through my son? I am going to be my son's son? I, the father, am going to be my son's son and he my father?"

"Of course. When you lived once before, he was your father and you were his son. So, you see, we are only repeating this once again."

The man ponders this and he looks at this entity and says, "But I love my wife. How am I going to be my wife's grandson?"

"From the time you are a small boy, you will adore your grandmother. By the time you are a man, she will have passed from the plane. Thus what has helped you to speak the love that is in your heart will have done its bidding; then it will be time to bring in new issues of seeing God in its beauty."

The man ponders this and he says, "Entity, who has helped me so much, when all has been made ready, I wish to become the child of my son."

The entity says to him, "The seed comes soon. When you see it, make yourself a part of your son's light."

"How do I do this?" And he looks around and, behold, to his amazement, the entity is gone. Instead he is looking at his son, for he has become a part of his son's light. Though his son knows not that he is there, feelings of his father have come more to mind recently. "If only my father could see me now," thinks his son. But of course his father does.

There comes a point when the child is within the womb. The man is going to be a part of the designing of this child through his thoughts and according to what he wishes his life to be. He may choose to take possession of the body upon conception or he may wait even till a year after birth to become the child.

The man is most anxious, for he is finding things most familiar to him. So he chooses quickly to become the child. Thus he thrusts forth himself and, in the twinkling of an eye, he has forgotten who he is. And the first thing he knows is the coughing in his throat and someone wiping his eyes and wrapping him in things that are ever so small.

This story that I have told to you is a truthful one. The entity of high regard and light did not choose for this master his life expression. He merely helped him to see it by taking him to a place, a magical pond, where his soul could be laid bare and he could review his life and determine from that the experiences he so needed.

Even as a young babe in that life, this entity already knew how to love. It was how to see God in himself and then become it that he had to master. And so he did. The entity's name was Buddha.

Always you have chosen. Always you have the will to choose. None choose for you. Had the man who lived in paradise not made an effort to become more and to see God through the beauty of this plane, he would still be on the fifth, and your world would not have been blessed by his great wisdom and light.

***

CHAPTER 7

Death Or Ascension

Death is not a necessary rule here. It is far easier to take your body with you. Then you do not have to be born in order to return here but can come and go at will.

Student: I recently found out that I'm going to have a baby and I would like to know, first of all, why is it that this baby chose to come to me. And how do we choose our parents?

Ramtha: How does anyone choose his parents in order to have a vehicle of expression? There are many reasons, many answers. But all who have passed from this plane and want to come back into this level are waiting for entities to bring forth children. Those who have given forth offspring in lives past always have genetic patterns of life — what you term parents — through which they can return.

Most will choose parents who are familiar to them, entities who have been children or parents to them in other lives. Yet there are entities who choose parents that they do not know, only because they provide a vehicle through which to express on this plane. For some, there is often no vehicle to come through when they desire to return, and they may have to wait hundreds of years before they find an available embodiment that suits them.

No one is really the mother or father of anyone else. All are sons and daughters of the Mother/Father Principle of life called God. All here are brothers and sisters to one another, siblings to one another. Your children and your parents are really siblings to you and an equal part of the mind of God.

Each entity knows before he comes here that he is not

coming back to be the grand beauty or the wealthy entity or the wretched pauper. He comes here because he wants to live here and to be enterprising in emotional learning on this level, to obtain emotional understandings that he wants to fulfill within his being. That is the true treasure of your life experiences, whether here or on other planes or dimensions, for that is the only thing that remains with you throughout eternity.

The entity who has chosen you, master, was what is termed your father's father's father. It is returning through the lineage which it set into motion over a century ago. Your desire to bear siblings enables it to come back, for now it has a vehicle through which it can return. The entity is in line, so to speak, for the fruit that you will bring forth. There are many entities in this audience who have entities surrounding them in their light field who are there waiting in line for conception to occur.

Student: Does that mean that it is a boy if it's my father's father's father?

Ramtha: Indeed. Do you approve?

Student: Oh, yes, very much. Ramtha, I have another question. Do we always have to be born through the birth canal in order to come back here?

Ramtha: To answer your question, master, first I wish you to understand that this is the plane of three-dimensional perception. It is the plane where thought is visible in the three-dimensional form called matter. This plane is the density of matter because thought has been expanded into a vibratory frequency called light, which then has been slowed in its vibratory frequency to become electrum, and from electrum to become gross matter, and from gross matter to become the solidity of this plane. The matter of this plane is thus light that has been slowed in its vibratory frequency and taken to its densest form.

In order for everything here to have the same density, everything has to vibrate at the same frequency. Thus your body is vibrating at the same frequency as the chair in which you are seated. This level exists to you because the senses of your embodiment have been designed to perceive the slowest frequencies of light called matter.

Because you are in your essence a light energy that is of a greater vibratory frequency than the density of matter, if you did not possess an embodiment of matter you would pass through the matter of this plane. Thus the body is what allows you, through its density and sense organs, to perceive and experience and interact with the matter of this plane.

So if you wish to be a part of this frequency, you must inhabit and be a part of a manifested body. One way to have an embodiment is to be born through the birth canal. The only other way to have a body in order to experience this plane is to be born through the birth canal, wholly maintain the integrity of self, and activate the entirety of the organ called the brain. Once you have opened your brain capacity to full use, you can at will command the body to raise its vibratory frequency to the point where it goes out of the frequency level of matter and into the vibratory frequency of light. That is called ascension.

Ascension is simply the means of taking the entirety of your being into another dimension of your accepted consciousness. Death is certainly one way to get there, but that means allowing the structure of the embodiment to fall into age and decay and to be no longer. Then you are without the embodiment. Ascension is taking your embodiment with you.

Those who have ascended this plane have mastered the ultimate, which is death. They have learned how to raise, through the power of their thought, the vibratory frequency of the body's molecular structures to the point where the body is taken with them into a light existence, thus forever bypassing death.

Student: I'm not sure I understand how ascension enables you to return to this plane.

Ramtha: You see, master, when you take your body with you, the body can be raised and lowered upon any frequency level you choose. So if you choose to come back into this frequency, you never have to look for another body, with another ego, in order to exist in another life, with another family, in another country. You no longer have to be born again into this plane of limited thinking only to undergo the programming of social consciousness and have to fight for the expression of self in order to regain your knowingness. You do not have to learn all over again that the body can be restored to the purest light form from which it came. You do not have to learn again that this is just an illusion and a game.

Once you master ascension, you maintain your body forever and can come and go at will with your own embodiment. Then any moment you wish to be a part of this plane again, all you have to do is lower the bodily vibrations to where it vibrates at the same frequency as this plane, and here you are.

All here are capable of ascending, for that which lurks behind the illusion of flesh is the creator of all universes. And you at your own choosing, through unlimited thinking, can make this manifestation occur. When you learn to master judgment against your thoughts and allow yourself to receive all thought, you have the power and the ability to become any ideal that you envision. Then you can do or become anything through thought. You can take your thought, concentrate it on the body, and command the body to vibrate faster. The body will then elevate towards the ideal that the thought holds steadfast for it. The whole of the body will begin to vibrate at a greater rate of speed. As it does so, the temperature of the body will rise and the body will begin to take on a glow. As it continues to vibrate faster, the matter of the body will go into pure light and then into pure thought. Then that which was seen is seen no longer.

Student: It would seem that ascension is a difficult thing to achieve because you don't hear much about people ascending.

Ramtha: On the contrary, master, ascension is very easy to achieve. In truth, it is simpler than dying. What is difficult to achieve is mastering judgment against your thoughts. What is indeed difficult to achieve is mastering the illusion of time in order to allot yourself the patience to do it. But once you do, ascension is simply a thought away. Then you have retained your body for all times and can thus be a traveler upon any plane at any moment you choose.

Student: And you never experience death?

Ramtha: Never. How can you when you are beyond it? You know, death is a great illusion. Death is an accepted reality on this plane, which all think must be; thus it has become a reality. Entity, the only reality is life; everything else is an illusion. Illusions are thoughts, that are games, that become realities.

Death is not a necessary rule in this kingdom. It is far easier to take the body with you. Then you never have to be born again through the birth canal and come into a consciousness, which regretfully does not accept your memory.

Student: So we don't have to die?

Ramtha: No one has to die. You will die only if you believe you will. But the body need not ever die. The Gods who designed it did not design it to last for only a fleeting moment in time. They designed the body to live off its glands, not its organs. And through a flow of hormones from the glands, the body was designed to live hundreds of thousands of years and never grow old. That was how it was programmed in its cellular structures. Only a short time ago in your history, entities lived to be thousands of years old.

Death is only the ending of the body, not of the personality self. But it is through the attitudes of the personality self that the life force of the body is degraded and the body is evoked into what is termed death.

Your body responds only to what it is told to do. Your soul, which sits beside your heart, governs the entire body through its emotional structure. The soul is what causes hormones to be dispensed throughout the body in order to maintain life in the embodiment. The soul does not do this on its own but rather under the direction of your attitudes and thought processes. Because of your attitudes here, the hormones cease to be created in the body after puberty. When they are no longer created, a death hormone is activated in the body and the whole body begins to break down, to grow old, and to die. The death hormone is activated in the body because you live in guilt and self-judgment and the fear of death. And to you, beauty is based wholly on the appearance of youth, not on the character of one's being. You anticipate death by purchasing insurance to bury yourself. You purchase insurance to protect your treasury if you become ill or diseased. You are doing everything possible to hasten the aging and death of your embodiment because you wholly expect it.

The body is only a servant, an instrument of collective thought. It is a magnificent creation, the most refined instrument there is. But it was not created to have a mind of its own. It was created specifically to be a servant, and it will live only as long as you allow it to live. If you accept thoughts of old age — expecting the body to wither away and die — or deny yourself love and happiness and joy, your body will gradually descend itself into the corruption of death.

You know, master, in this very moment you can cease time completely and live in the foreverness of this Now, if you so choose, for is time not an illusion? Who has seen it? A great hypocrisy exists here because you refuse to believe in the unseen, yet you wholly worship and are enslaved to time.

You have the power right within you, right where you are, to reverse the age of your embodiment back into youth and to live on and on and on. How? Simply through your attitude. If you do not want the body to age and die, change your attitude. Let your attitude say that the body will live forever, and so it will. Remove all things from your life that acknowledge the ending of it, and it will never end. Never have the word "old" in your vocabulary understanding. Have "forever" in your understanding. Cease the celebration of your birthdays, for that only gives credence to the aging process. If it pleases you to acknowledge your birth, do so, but reverse the count of your years and become younger. When you do not expect your death, you will never know it.

Always live in the present. Never acknowledge any future other than this Now. Your Now will be eternity if you permit it to be so. Never contemplate how long you are going to live, for you will always live. Contemplate the foreverness of your body, and so it will become. That is simply how it is.

Love yourself, master. Bless your body. Speak to your soul, which is the lord of your being, and command it to bring forth the enzymes of youth, and it will. Know that the body can live forever. And how does it live forever? By telling it to.

Immortality is achieved only when one does away with the understanding of mortality. This travesty called death could be eliminated by the whole lot of humanity if they lived not in the future or the past but in the ongoingness of this Now and if the attitude of living was greater than the prospects of dying. This shall be eliminated here in the years to come, for time will be no longer and these understandings will have become a living reality in everyone upon your plane. Then death will have become a senseless no-thing.

Student: I have another question about ascension. Is ascension what Jesus did when he resurrected his body and then reappeared?

Ramtha: That is indeed how Yeshua ben Joseph did it. That is what I did. That is what Buddha did. That is what Osiris, Omeka, Yukad, and Rackabia did. And there have been thousands more that you are not even aware of.

Student: Is ascension something that you foresee many of us accomplishing in this lifetime?

Ramtha: Very few will ascend in this life, for few will truly realize and appreciate what is being taught here. Most will die because they acknowledge age and deterioration, and they care for the splendid machine that carries them only to the extent that it looks good. Thus they will age and the body will fall into corruption, and it will die. Then the Spirit and soul shall be freed of their union with the body. However, in order to come back to this plane of density in matter, they will need a vehicle through which to express; thus is the rebirthing of masters.

Most here will die. But that does not mean that that is all for them. It simply means that the mask of the embodiment is removed and they will have to take up another. But if they do choose to return here, they will be returning to a consciousness that will facilitate ascension, for soon it will be an understood and accepted reality.

Student: Is there anything I can do or take for my body that will help my baby?

Ramtha: The only thing that you need do in regard to your body, master, is don't worry about how it looks. Know that it is beautiful at all times, and your baby will feel the same when it emerges. No matter how large you have gotten, it will be a happy soul. You have learned?

Student: Much. Thank you.

Ramtha: And, master, when you rear your sibling, never tell it that life will be sweeter when it grows up. That is a very limiting thing to do to another entity. Create the understanding that every moment of its life is important. Allow your child to grow slowly and to be a child as long as it desires to be. Then you will be a wondrous blessing to one of your beloved brothers and can share in its joy of this plane. So be it.

***

CHAPTER 8

Creation And Evolution

*You are the only creation that is directly of God.
Everything else you have created by thinking and
feeling it into being.*

Who set the lights into the heavens? Who designed the loveliness of flowers and the magnificence of trees? And who created the enigma and the wonderment called man? 'Twas not God, the totality of life. It was you, the Gods, the wonderful sons of an all-loving Father who created all that is — all. The Father is the substance, the thought mass from which all things come. But you who possess the capacity to think, and the capacity to feel, and the divine essence of free will, are the supreme creators in life.

God is indeed the totality of thought, the source of everything that is. But you are the ones who have taken from the thought that the Father is and created all the splendor and loveliness of created form. Through your creative power and your sovereign godship, you have the ability to accept, to hold, and to contemplate thought. And through that intelligence you have fashioned everything that is.

Ponder for a moment a fantasy. Think of a fantasy that is exciting, thrilling, volatile to your being. Now feel all the emotion of that fantasy. That is how your universe was created. That is how man was created. That is how everything is created.

My beloved masters, you are indeed the creators of all life. You are the ones who made the spectacular lights that you see in your heavens. You are the ones who created the realities of color, design, texture, and smell. You are indeed the magnificent creatures of a magnificent Father that is truly everything that is. You are not the bastards of the universe; you are the creators of it. You are the supreme intelligence of God expressing in your own creation called man, and all life stands awaiting your presence, your thought, your feeling.

You, my esteemed brothers, are eminent creatures of divine proportions who hold latent within your beings the intelligence and the power to create all things, and yet you do not realize this. You are more than creatures of flesh. You are awesome entities expressing through form in order to continue the creative abilities within you.

Without your creative thought processes, your superb intelligence, and the profound emotion within your souls — without all that is unseen about you — you would be a no-thing. And without your creative abilities, life would be a no-thing, for thought could not propagate itself to become the values of life or the eternity that is yet to be lived.

Without your creative value, nothing would be recognized for what it is. What would be the reason for the life and the beauty of a flower if there were no one to appreciate its loveliness? It would have no meaning here without you.

Without you, this place of yours would be only a formless planet wallowing in the sperms of creativity. Without you, the seasons never would have been, the flowers never would have bloomed, the sun never would have risen, and the winds never would have blown, for you created this kingdom according to your purposeful designs, and all things have come forth willingly to glorify the God that lies within you.

Who else designed this magnificent place for you to inhabit? Only you did this. Are you not the creatures of supreme intelligence? Indeed you are. You did not evolve into that. You have always been that.

Now I am here to teach you to become unlimited, indeed, but I will teach you of your worth and value first. To know that you are divine, to understand the supreme intelligence and awesome power that you possess, it is important for you to understand your heritage. It is important for you to understand how you became, in your beginning, wisps of light of awesome power and how you have evolved yourselves to become the enigma called man. I will thus begin to explain.

In your Book of Books it says, "In the beginning was the Word, and all was with the Word." Most improper. The word was nothing without the thought, for thought is the basis and creator of everything that is.

In the beginning — what you would term the beginning — all was the infiniteness of thought. Now the infiniteness of thought I will call God the Father. What you term God is, in a more unlimited understanding, thought, the principal cause and foundation of all life. Everything that is, that ever has been, that ever will be, is derived from thought, the intelligence that is the mind of God.

So in the beginning there was the infinite space of thought. And God always would have been thought without form had he not contemplated himself, turned and bent inward unto himself the thought that he was. When the Father contemplated the thought that he was, he expanded himself into a unique form of himself, for any time a thought is contemplated, the action of pure reasoning expands the thought. The thought becomes more; it becomes greater. Thus the Father, who had never before expanded his being, contemplated himself into a greaterness.

What gave the Father the desire to comprehend himself into a greater existence? Love. The very essence, the very purpose of contemplative thought is love. It was the love of God for itself that gave it the desire to contemplate itself into a unique, expanded form of itself.

From that movement of love, all of you were born, for when God embraced and loved itself into a greaterness, all of you became that which God expanded itself into. Each of you became in that same wondrous moment an illustrious part of the first contemplated, expanded thought.

Being the first created unit of God the Father, each of you became a God of God, a son of the Father, and a part of the divine intelligence called the mind of God. You, the Gods, are the only creation that is directly of God. You are the only creation that is ever the complete duplicate of what the Father is, for you are the Father in an expanded form of himself. All that the Father is, he is infinitely in the composite of his beloved sons.

God the Father is compulsive, contemplative thought called life, an ongoingness that can never stand still any more than your own thoughts can. In order for thought or life to be an ongoing expansion into forever, it must have a reason to continue. The reason is you. Each of you became a part of the mind of God so that, through you, life would continue to expand itself into forever — which indeed has no measure in time — for forever is in this moment. It is the ongoingness and the eternity of Now.

For the purpose of going onward, the Father gave each of you the only thing that ever is or ever will be: the totality of thought, which is the totality of God. Each of you were given by the Father, for the Father, all that you are: a divine intelligence and a sovereign, creative will. Through that intelligence and freedom of will, you were given the power to take from the thought that the Father is and expand yourself according to your own contemplative thought processes.

God, the divine mind, continuously expands itself and becomes more through each of you. Whatever you become in your own expansion, the Father readily becomes. And whatever the Father has come to be — through the expansion of all of his beloved sons — you may readily become, for each son stands in receivership of whatever the Father is. Thus through your contemplative thoughts, you can always be what God is: an ongoing, expansive, extraordinarily wonderful kingdom.

When thought contemplated itself in your beginning, what it expanded itself into was the principle of thought called light. Light was created first because whenever thought is contemplated and expanded, it is always lowered into a vibratory frequency that emits light. Light is thus the first lowered form of contemplated, expanded thought.

Your original heritage goes back to the birthing of light, for each particum of light born of the first contemplated thought became an individual, a God, a son. Thus all became what is termed lightbeings at the birthing of creation.

Everyone was created into being at that same moment. All entities that ever were, or ever will be, were created from thought into light the moment God contemplated itself. The light emanating from the space of thought became adjacent to and part of the mind of God, the flow of all thought, termed the river of thought.

The light that each of you became was and is the intelligence that you are; it is God in its expanded form as light. That divine light, which is your original and permanent body, is the Spirit of your being or what I call the God of your being, for your Spirit is God, the mind of God in singular form. To this day you still possess the original Spirit, the original God-self, the original body of light that you became in all of your glory the moment thought, your beloved Father, contemplated and expanded itself into light.

Now in your beginning when thought, or God, passed through the Spirit of your being, an emotion was created but it was fleeting. So your soul was created through your creative force in order to capture the river of love that issued forth from God the Father. It was created for the purpose of captivating thought from the ongoing flow of the river of thought and putting it into a stillness — what is termed memory — in the form of emotion.

Your soul, which is housed within your Spirit, is what has enabled you to be a creative principle. For in order to create, you must have the ability to hold the image of thought clear and steadfast in memory. By doing so, you can contemplate the thought and expand it into the creative values that you call reality.

For instance, in order to create a new and unique flower, you must have the thought of a flower emerge. The thought of a flower is taken from the flow of ongoing thought, which the Spirit or light of your being is at one with. The thought is then held clear in the soul as an image, in the form of emotion. Through desire, you can now recall the image of the thought "flower," contemplate it, and expand it into whatever unique form, color, or height you desire. Now you can uniquely create a flower however you wish and at any moment you wish. By holding the thought perfectly still in memory, you may paint its picture perfectly.

Without your soul, you could not expand the Father into created form, for you could not make thought stand still in order to contemplate and expand it into creation.

Now what you term creation is really the value of life that has always been. There is no beginning to creation and certainly there is no ending to it. And the creators from the substance of thought are all of you, the light entities, the Gods. Everything has been created by the sons from the thought that the Father is, and whatever the sons create becomes the expanded self of the Father.

Everything that you see around you is called matter. The Father is the matter, for everything is God. But the creators and designers of the matter are the artisans of artisans which all of you are, Gods that you are, for you had from your beginning the purposeful intelligence to create into matter whatever ideals you could envision through thought.

Everything is derived from thought — everything. Each thing of matter has come forth from a thought that was embraced into emotion to form an ideal of creation. Before anything was ever created, the thought of it was first envisioned through the soul as an ideal. All things of matter were created from a thought ideal envisioned by the Gods and put together by them from the matter that the Father is.

Now all matter is surrounded by light. Your scientists are beginning to suspect — and they are correct in their suspicion — that if you take light and lower or slow its vibratory frequency, it becomes gross matter. And where did the light come from? Thought, God.

Whenever you contemplate thought and emotionally embrace it, the thought expands into the vibratory frequency of light. If you slow the movement of the particles of light and condense it, you create electrum, an electromagnetic field that has positive and negative poles, which you call electricity. If you slow and condense the thought still further, beyond the electromagnetic fields, the electrum coagulates into gross matter. Gross matter then coagulates into the molecular and cellular structures called form. And the form is held together by the thought that the soul envisioned as an ideal of creation.

All things are created by taking that which has no speed — thought — and expanding it into that which does — light — and then slowing the light down until you create this and that and all that is around you.

Beloved masters, it is you who have created through your own thought processes the beauty and the splendor of all that is. It is you who have created all things — from thought, into light, into electrum, into matter, into form — simply by thinking and feeling them into being, for you, who were thought that had been lowered into light, contemplated the light you had become and loved the light that you were and, by doing so, you lowered light one step further to create electrum. When you contemplated the electrum that God had become through your thought processes, you lowered the electrum into gross matter, or coagulated thought, the lowest form of thought and yet another dimension of the Father into himself.

So your first movement was the recognition of what is termed the science of thought into matter. And that science was never taught; it was simply understood, for it was a process of life that you were involved in. It was from that science, from that understanding, that created forms began.

In the beginning of created forms, the Gods contemplated themselves, the lights that they were, and created the ideal of light into matter by creating what are called suns. And there were a trillion billion of them without number. All of the suns were created from the focusing or the fusion of gaseous matter that resulted from the lowering of electrum. And from the great suns, the central sparks of life, rotating spheres called planets were created and thrust into their orbits. And upon the spheres, the Gods created designs. And it took eons for you to learn design.

Who created this universe and all universes that surround an even greater sun cycle? You did, indeed. You designed it simply. Each thing that you created through contemplated thought expanded your experience, which allowed feelings, the truest treasure of thought, to occur within your soul. And it was through feelings that the plane of matter was created.

Your divinity lies in that you are indeed the beginning sparks of light and that you, the creators, have created from the Father through your sovereign wills all that is — all. God did not create the universes; he is the universes. You created them from your thinking processes by feeling them in your souls.

Most of you were among the Gods who came to this place of yours called Earth eons ago, and here you created and evolved all life. Over millions of years, as you know time to be, you took from the thought that the Father is and, through your supreme intelligence and creative power, you designed your ideals of creation.

You, the light entities, formulated living organisms here from bacteria that formed through the reaction of gaseous matter in water. That was the clay from which you created the different values of life. And in the beginning your creations were merely grouped matter expressing as a glob of something. Your creativity was very simple because you were only beginning to understand the reality of matter and how to create from it. But over eons of time you created the plants and animals and every other living creature upon this plane.

Creatures were devised by you as an expression of your creative emotion, as an expression of creative life, life forms that could be mobile and that could themselves express. The flower was created by a group of you. Color was introduced. Aroma was added. Later, various aspects of the flower were brought into different designs.

You must understand that you did not labor to create these things, for as lightbeings you were without an embodiment to labor with. Whatever you desired to create, you simply became it. In order to give substance to matter — to give personality to it, to give intelligence and design to it —you became a part of everything you created. Once each creation became a living thing of the intelligence of its creator, you withdrew from your creation, always searching for greater creations.

Everything you created here would not be so beautiful or sublime, nor would it have purposeful meaning, if it did not have the breath of life of its creator within it. You are the ones who breathed into your creations the intelligence or patterns of genetic memory called instinct. That is what gave your creations a purpose for being and the means — through reproductive processes and the sharing of genes — for new species to evolve. Yet the new species would still carry the intelligence of instinct, the breath of life from the great creative Gods who set into motion the patterns for evolution. That is why all living things have within them the divine essence that is the spark of life from you, the Gods, their creators.

It was not until a food chain had been clearly established here that the Gods decided to create a vehicle of matter through which they could experience their creations and continue to express their creativity, but as themselves rather than through their creations. And for that they created the embodiment called man.

Now thought is a penetrating frequency, an essence that passes through matter. Thus the Gods, who were thought in the form of light, could become the flower, yet never smell it, never know its essence. They were like the breeze that would blow through the trees, yet could never feel or embrace the tree. They would pass through stone, yet they could not feel it because thought is not affected by the matter that the stone is, for it lacks the sensitivity to feel the essence of a lower vibration.

In order for the Gods to smell the flower, to hold the flower, to wear the flower — in order for them to know its beauty and experience its vividness — they had to create a vehicle of matter that vibrates at the same rate of speed that the flower is vibrating. Thus the embodiment called man was created, after all other things were created, so that the Gods could feel and experience their creations and express their creative ability through gross matter — or what is termed solidity in mass — thought taken to its lowest form.

Man was created through a thought ideal to be a vehicle for the Gods to ride within. It was the perfect embodiment for a

God, for it could hold the soul and be enveloped by the Spirit of
the God. Now through an embodiment, the Gods could touch the
flower and smell its essence, and the experience of that would be
recorded forever in their souls as feelings, the treasure of their
doings. Now indeed they could look upon a tree and contemplate
it, savor its smell, and touch its beauty. Now the Gods could see
and touch and embrace and speak to one another. Now they could
nurture and observe and be completely volatile to one another.
And now the Gods, as man, had a whole new adventure in matter
in which to play for the invisible essence called feelings.

Thus the Gods, lightbeings without the density of mass,
created a density appropriate to their ideal. Through the mass
of the embodiment they could express in yet another reality:
thought manifested into the form called matter. In that, they
became God, divine thought manifested into the intelligence of
the cellular mass called mankind. Thus they became God/man,
man/God: God expressing in the wonderment of human form;
man expressing the God within him to continue his Father's
expansion into forever.

The first men came forth only after much experimentation
by a group of the Gods. At first only males were created, and
they were not even created with loins. The loins were inside of
them so that they could reproduce themselves through the process
called cloning. Thus all man embodiments looked alike when
they were first created. And they were rather humble creatures
who would be considered very grotesque to you today. But to the
Gods in those times, they were very beautiful. Unfortunately,
they were not very swift on their feet; thus they were continuously
made a meal of by the animals about. So the Gods tried and
tested and modified them for a long time until they were
worthy of complete possession. Once the embodiment had
been perfected, many of the Gods in great jubilation took
possession of embodiments for a new adventure in the
exploration of life.

The embodiments that the Gods inhabited were designed
to house a power structure that would enable the lightbeings to
improve continuously upon the embodiment so they could live

and coexist in a very dangerous environment. The body was designed so that the memory of every thought the God embraced into emotion would be patterned in every cell and thus carried on through the process of cloning.

When womb of man or woman was created much later, as a more perfected form of man, it permitted uniqueness and further refinement of the embodiment through the sharing of genes. The man would carry in his seed the patterns of his understanding gained to that point, and the woman would carry it in her egg. Through the act of copulation, the genetic patterns of the two would come together to create an even greater entity based on the learning and realizations of its parents. Yet they were creating only a better body through this process, not a better Spirit.

As the understanding of the Gods living as man began to grow — as their survival necessitated it — the body was continuously perfected from its primeval form, or what you call evolved, a process which has continued for over ten and one-half million years in your counting. It has taken that long for you to become what you are this moment.

Your body is young. Man, in the uprightness of his tested mobility, is only ten and one-half million years old. But you, the lightbeings, have always been, because how does one determine the beginning of contemplative thought based on time when there wasn't anything called time. So you are ancient. And for billions of years, as you term and measure time, you created in electrum. Then lowering electrum into gross matter became a new and different adventure. Thus through billions of years of design and exploration, man became a living, breathing creature of coagulated thought and dense matter.

All of this plane you created. That is why reality would not be here if it weren't for the lot of you. The animals are beloved, for they have been given the breath of life through you, their creators. The flowers are beloved, for they have the patterns of your beauty in them. All life does, and it is all because of you.

Who are you? You are the great Gods of light, the great creators of all life. You are the grand, infinite thought magnified and lowered into creative matter. You are God, the forever thought, experiencing the form called humanity. You are God manifested as man to continue the expansion of thought into forever.

Student: I find myself in a position of having to decide whether or not I'm going to pursue the learning of all the things you are teaching. All that you say pleases me, but I'm held back by an element of doubt as to whether all the things you teach are true. Is there anything you can tell me or do for me which will convince me that what you say is true?

Ramtha: No. But I will ask you this: Tell me what is not truth.

Student: What is not truth? Well, for example, I recently heard a tape recording of an audience in which you gave a very beautiful description of how creation began. It was very pleasing and very detailed, especially in comparison to other versions I've heard. I'd like to believe that the way you spoke it was exactly the way it happened. But I can't be sure that what you said is true.

Ramtha: Then how did it happen?

Student: I don't have an explanation. I'm just searching for a better understanding.

Ramtha: You have heard many explanations of how creation occurred. Which do you choose?

Student: I've really only heard two or three. But yours pleases me the most.

Ramtha: Why?

Student: Well, it is more detailed.

Ramtha: How could it be so detailed? How does one have knowledge of the things they speak?

Student: Experience.

Ramtha. Ah, indeed. That was my experience of how it was and how it is. That is how I remember it.

Student: But can you understand my doubts?

Ramtha: Indeed, because you have not allowed yourself to remember. But I will tell you this: Listen to it again, and while all the other accounts have utterly failed to explain anything, there is no lacking in this account, and it all follows suit.

Convince you? I will not do that, for I would never convince you. Only you allow that to occur.

Student: Well, can I ask you a couple of questions for clarification?

Ramtha: Indeed.

Student: You have said that the Father expands through us. Does that mean that the divine mind is actually growing through us, through our creations?

Ramtha: Indeed. For the Father was, in your beginning, the Void without form, space without light. And he always would have been that had he not contemplated himself and embraced the thought that he was. When he did that, he expanded himself into light, the first expansion of thought. Of that light, all of us became. Why? To continue the expansion of the Father into forever. How? Through the same process of contemplation that the Father began in the birthing of our light forms.

From the splendid moment of our soul's birth, each of us began to evolve and expand ourselves. Our souls enabled us to captivate thought and hold it in the form of emotion. Through that we could go inward, contemplate the thought, and expand it into creativity. That is what allowed the world to come into being, the flower to be a seed into a bloom, and the animals to become and roam.

Thought, your beloved Father, is of itself unmanifested emotion. Thought is not given credence as being until it is manifested as emotion within the soul. Once the thought is embraced and recorded in the soul, then it becomes real. Then it has design. Then it has structure. Then it has pertinence.

Who created everything that you see here? 'Twas not God, the thought. It was you, the Gods, the emotion, who took thought and felt it into the lowered forms of matter. What you term reality does not become that until a thought is embraced into emotion within the soul to form an ideal of creation and then expressed as created form. It is feelings and the values of emotion that give thought credence and the form that you call reality. That is how the Father grows every moment.

Created form is thus the evolution of thought into emotion. That is what allows matter to be created. That is what allows you to create, to evolve, to become, to express, to do whatever you choose to do. And you have never been judged by the life force that allows you to be what you are, for in being what you are, you expand and give credence to the mind of God.

The Father not only works through you but feels through you, is through you. You are that which he is, and that reality is being re-created every moment. That is why everything you do, that you have ever done, has always been accepted in the eyes of God.

Everything here, which is born of thought and light, you created. Thus the kingdom of heaven, the kingdom of God, has been expanded through his beloved sons, you, himself. So love what you are immensely, for you are a beautiful thing who has created all things for the joy of it.

Student: Thank you, Ramtha. I have one other question. You said that man has been here for ten and a half million years. But as I understand it, scientists have evidence that man has been here for only about a million years, perhaps two million at most.

Ramtha: For you to understand, your archaeologists have a way to date things based on the radioactivity of that which they find. What gives those things radioactivity is the light principle called your sun. Yet the light from your sun did not directly bombard this plane for as long as your scientists believe, for your planet was surrounded by water for a long time. The water was your oceans, which were still in the atmosphere at that time. When light from your sun hit the water in the stratum, the water diffused the light; thus there was diffused light everywhere. Thus no thing was exposed to radiation as it is this day. Yet they determine the age of man through the radioactivity of that which they find, believing that the sun's rays had direct access to this plane for longer than they really did.

The Gods have been here as man for ten and one-half million years in many forms of the embodiment in order to perfect it. And what I have just given you is a clue for you to contemplate so that you may reason this for yourself.

Now tell me, master, why do you choose this creation story over the others? Do you know why?

Student: Simply because the explanation pleases me.

Ramtha: But why does it please you?

Student: Because you speak that we are all perfect, that no one is less than anyone else, and that life is ongoing.

Ramtha: Indeed. And it would also mean that everything your religions have taught could be wrong. Do you know what is wonderful about that? It means that perhaps there really is no such thing as a devil, or hell, or sin, or damnation, or a fearsome God; that they could be wrong. And they are.

***

CHAPTER 9

Higher Than Angels

To be a part of humanity is a holy experience, for when you become humanity you are wholly experiencing God.

You are really rather splendid, every one of you, for you are volatile, creative, unique, and indeed divine. Though you have been taught that you are wretched creatures, what really matters is how you are known in the understanding called life. And in that understanding you are known as beloved of God the Father, for you are an eternal part of the mind of God. You have yet to realize how precious you truly are, but you will.

Who you are to me is a beloved brother — and not only to me but to all entities, seen and unseen, in all universes and in all levels of life — for we are all linked together through the grace, the intelligence, and far greater through the love of that which is termed God, the wondrous thought that supports and holds you throughout all eternity, regardless of all your outrageous endeavors.

You are a grander treasure than you know, for without even one of you, life and universes and molecular structures would never have existed. For you and because of you, life has become an exuberant display of the intelligence — of the drama, if you will — of the continuation of the patterns of thought into the brilliant colors of reality. You are precious indeed for, regardless of how you think of yourselves, you have added to the spectacular display of the totality of all that is.

Splendid you are, for look at the lot of you who comprise

humanity. In the semblance of your countenances there is not one of you who looks like another. You are like the flowers of a magnificent garden whose seeds pollinate and create new flowers that are evermore beautiful and lush in their deepening hues. Each of you is beautiful, yet different, for each of you is God expressing through the uniqueness of your own willful, creative designs.

All of you were once wisps of thought, emanating light, who became the continuation of God into the ongoingness of forever. In order to erect a greater kingdom for exploration, you designed with great care and much experimentation embodiments of matter or, if you will, coagulated thought. Through your embodiments you were able to express yourselves upon yet another plane of existence and thus explore the whole of the patterns of thought called God. Thus in your adventures into infinite creativity, you who were once light without form have transformed yourselves into the cellular matter called mankind. In that, you became God/man, the intelligence called the mind of God expressing through the living organism called man.

As mankind you are a remarkable intelligence. You have not only breathed into your own cellular structures the breath of life and the instinctual means to survive but, for divine purposes, you have integrated your supreme intelligence with the matter of the embodiment for the purpose of refining and evolving it. Through your design of a science of evolution, you have thus evolved yourselves from what is termed Neanderthal to what is called Homo sapiens, humanity. Thus has mankind become on this plane — over eons of time and through much experimentation, evolution, and many traumas — the erect entities who now sit before me.

All of you are here upon what is termed the plane of demonstration in order to demonstrate the power of your creative intelligence in this level of life, a great level of life, for here thought, your beloved Father, exists in all forms of its manifestation: from light all the way to the density of matter.

Do you know that intelligence thrives in all places? It does indeed. But here upon this place of yours called Earth is where humanity — the marriage of thought with matter — is at its peak of evolution.

You, humanity, do you think you are backward? Do you think you are less than those who are in the unseen? You are not. You are on a grand adventure into the understanding of the whole of your eternal thought processes. Without becoming God in the form called humanity, you could never understand the conclusiveness that God is — no one could — for the kingdom of God is expansive from light into electrum, into matter, into form. Thus God is not only the higher frequencies of thought; it is also the densest and lowest frequency of thought called gross matter.

Only when you have become humanity do you express what the Father is in all forms of thought, for when you are God/man, God/woman, not only are you thought and emotion and evolving will but you are light, you are electrum, you are matter in the form called flesh and blood. No one expresses the whole of God's kingdom until he becomes God in the form called man.

To understand the totality of your thought processes — to embrace the whole of who and what you are, God that you are — you must be pliable enough and love yourself enough to embark upon all planes of existence, including this one. Once you have lived and expressed upon the plane of gross matter, then you will have an understanding of God in the form called matter.

Those who have yet to become God/man do not have the complete experience of God to reflect upon in order to gain the wisdom and understanding of all life. Only the ones who travel to this plane to become a part of the splendor of this plane — to evolve it, to move mountains, to create color, to create monuments of dignity — only they understand the intricacies of love, of joy, of creation. Only those travelers, which you are, are the ones who have gained the understanding of forever and the desire to pursue it, for they are the ones who create forever for all of life, for as long as there is a plane of matter, it permits the ongoingness of life into infinite creativity. Thus to be man and woman, to be collective humanity, is indeed a privilege. It is an honor. It is indeed divine life.

There is a term you have called angels, and there are many of you who desire to be such a divine creature. But there is a great holdback in being an angel because they have no reasoning balance, for they have yet to live as man. They are simply energy, the Gods who will eventually become God/man, but they do not have sympathy or compassion for mankind. How could anyone in the unseen completely understand you until they have been you? Mankind is far greater advanced than angels, for they have no understanding of God living in the limited form called man; thus they are limited in their understanding of mankind and his joys and sorrows.

I tell you, to be a part of humanity is a holy experience, for when you become humanity, you are wholly experiencing God. Only when you become humanity have you journeyed to the perimeters that encompass the entirety of the kingdom of heaven.

So you have not degraded yourselves by becoming humanity — you must understand that — because if you have never been the human element, you can never completely enter the kingdom of heaven. How can you ascend into heaven if you have never descended into life?

It is worthy; it is worthwhile. It is wise to become man in order to understand this fire that lives within you called God Almighty. All life is composed of this fire, and experiencing it through the supreme intelligence of gross matter — what is called mankind — allows you the complete view of what God is. And when you understand completely all that God is — inner and outer space, matter, flesh and blood, love and joy and sorrow — then you will be all that the Father is.

Now the reason you are upon this plane is to continue the exploration of God through the density of the embodiment in which you are living. That which supports your creative evolvement is called life, the same life force that holds an atom in its sphere and your earth in space. And that life force has one universal principle: to be ever-evolving, ever-expanding, ever-becoming. Your life's purpose for all time has been to experience life and learn from it and to refine and integrate what you have learned back into the principle called life.

This that you are living is called creation. You are playing with creative thought and expressing it through matter for the purpose of gaining wisdom, understanding, and identifying the great mystery of yourself. Yet all of this plane is a grand illusion. Everyone thinks that the three-dimensional plane is the reality, but it is not. All the games that mankind plays are illusions — they are dreams — for this reality can be dreamt away. The real world is that which lies within you, the encounter with emotion each moment you feel. The real world exists only from the standpoint of emotion, not governed by logic but by moving love.

This world that you call reality would never exist if you did not have the eyes to perceive it through moving emotion within your soul, for it would be a no-thing. All of this paradise of matter was created simply to evoke emotion within the souls of those who participate in this wonderment of creativity. Why? For the greatest prize of life called wisdom. And wisdom is not an intellectual understanding; it is indeed an emotional understanding gained from experience.

Life, this grand stage, is your kingdom. It is the platform upon which you create your illusions. This wondrous stage affords you the opportunity to dream into existence any reality you desire. For the God that you are has the unlimited freedom to dream any thought, feel the emotion, and manifest the dream into a reality. And anywhere in between you can change your mind.

The reason for life on a plane of density is to prove to that which embarks upon it — and this is an experience exclusive to humanity — that with each turn of the thought embraced into emotion, the reality soon follows. And when that understanding is grasped, when that awesome power of creativity is realized, it quickens an alignment within you through which you know that you are God. Yet without the human experience, you could never know that.

This life is for you to embrace. It is full and rich with the fervor of adventure and challenge. It provides all around you open doors and opportunities for your involvement and evolvement in order for you to become. To become what? The cumulative whole of all experiences, which will equate to you simply that you are God, for only a God has the ability to create monuments in matter that testify to the glory of itself.

You are to be commended for being God/man, God/woman, for it is only when God becomes man that life upon this plane can be created and evolved. You are splendid indeed. You are more powerful than you know. Your every emotion, your every thought creates life. It is up to you to give life presence, to support all life to come. It is not for those who are in the unseen. Those in the unseen are ongoing in that understanding. But who is to support this material kingdom that is the emerald of all kingdoms? You, by how you think and how you embrace it.

You are the ones who give credence to everything. It is you who add to the platform called life. It is you who exalt and glorify this kingdom of God. You don't know that because you have always thought that you were a little lower than the angels. Hardly. You don't really know that yet but you will, because soon life and rainbows and colors and lights will become very much a reminder to you of who you really are. It is called the Age of Enlightenment and, in that time, what will life here have become? It will be understood as a necessary experience for one to unfold into the realization that he is indeed a part of the mind of God. Once you know that, then what of the adventures that await? You will have all of forever to play in. You will have all of the infiniteness of thought to reevaluate and reissue elements: matter, time, space, distance, you.

You are splendid indeed because you made a long journey into this sphere to become who you are now. And that journey has been for the purpose of knowing God in all that it is: from thought into light, into the divisions of electrum, into gross matter, into this plane. You all made that journey. That is not only splendid of you, it is also rather daring of you, and there is a bit of risk involved. There is a great possibility, through the transfiguration of the great immortal self into the material plane, of losing one's identity and becoming wholly embroiled in survival. And, alas, that is what most of humanity has done.

Do you know why you have ventured to listen to me, enigma that I am? Because you know that what I have just told you is a truth, and you are seeking the path that leads back to the first divine knowingness that set all of this into motion. Deep within you, you know that you are more than collective matter, that you are more than flesh and blood, that you are really rather divine. And you are. You are here to realize that, to embrace the divine principle that you are, to find within you that there is the beginning light, the breath of thought that gave you life in your beginning.

My beautiful masters, you gave the wind life. You gave the sun a reason to be where it is. You gave the storm clouds a reason to muster their strength to nourish and quench the thirst of the earth. You don't know that because you have always considered yourselves less than the love of life that God truly is. I adore you, for I have been as you. I lived your illusions and I became your dreams. And where I went, one hour you too shall go, but you shan't ever go there until you have embraced this life and embraced God through the embrace of yourself.

I salute you from the depths of my being. You are indeed grand. You are indeed loved. You are indeed needed. You are indeed cherished. You are the reason for forever. You are indeed the reason for life.

***

CHAPTER 10

The Identifiable God

God can never be identified outside of yourself. To even attempt it is unfair to yourself because you are going outside of what you are to describe something which emanates from within you.

Each of you is upon this plane for many reasons, but the grandest reason of all and of utmost importance is to understand and love the greatest mystery of all, the point called self. And that point I refer to appropriately as God the Father within you, that which gave you credence in your beginning, that which you create and evolve through, and that which you will once again become.

Since you are to become as God is — to express completely the God within you — just what is it that you are to become? What is the identity of God that will give you a point of reference to thus become? Well, let us see.

This God that I love, that I am a servant unto, that all wonders are worked through, is the ongoingness of the totality of life. In the ongoingness of the kingdom of life, which is the ongoingness of eternity, the Now is all there ever is. In this Now, this specific moment, God is all things that are being as they are. Thus in this Now, God is the Isness of all that is. And in the Nows to come, God is the pulsating of all life ongoing abreast of itself — vibrantly living, feeling, expanding, evolving — expressing the beingness of itself.

God is the conclusiveness of all things that are, and yet it is without borders, without beginning, and without ending. It is the infiniteness that has no parallel. The Isness of God is reality upon reality, dimension upon dimension, universe upon universe.

You have one little galaxy here. And if you think that you are the only life that exists in it, you are rather arrogant. In your Milky Way alone there are ten billion suns, and with each sun there are planets that are supporting life.

There is no number in counting to tell you how many solar systems there are. None. There is no number in counting to tell you of every planet, great and small, and the life that dwells therein. There is no number. And if you wish to comprehend infinity, you had best reprogram your thinking to perceive beyond time, distance, and measure, for in a greater reality, none of these exist.

God is. When was the beginning? There never was one. God always was the thought, the space, the Void that supports and gives life to the Telstars. Know you what a Telstar is? It transforms light into matter and spews it forth into the universe to create stellar systems. Where did the Telstar come from? Thought, God, space, the great Void, where you look out and see stars and forever. If you want to visualize God in its impeccable and infinite being, visualize the open-ended eternity called space, for space is the river of thought that surrounds everything you see, that supports and gives credence to everything that is.

Everyone talks about space as if it were nothing. But what is the power that allows all things to steadfast themselves into orbital systems? What is it that holds up your earth in the Void? What supports your Milky Way, which has ten billion suns in it? What holds it up? What causes your sun to be held in position? What allows the passage of all matter? What indeed is the highway that light travels upon? You say nothing? Show me a no-thing that can support ten billion suns and their solar systems.

God is on one level the matter that makes up the substance of all things. On another level it is the time flow of the different dimensions, the time warp that creates parallel universes. On another level it is the spectrum called light that gives supportiveness to matter. And on the greatest level of all, it is the no-thing that holds you into position: thought, the foreverness of space.

God is the whole of life — pulsating, expanding, evolving — ongoing into forever. It is the Isness that allows what was, the permeance of what is, and the promise of what is to come. It is the movement that endows life, the unlimited thought process that reaches no goals or ideals but is continuously creating life from thought, into light, into matter. God is the essence of all that is in a motivated force that is ever-changing, ever-creating, ever-expanding, ever-being.

How can you identify that which is all-encompassing, all-powerful, ever-evolving, ever-moving, ever-allowing, ever-being? How can you say this is what God is, when what God is now will not be the same in the next Now? How do you perceive an open-ended universe?

With a finite, thinking mind you cannot identify that which is beyond time, distance, space, and matter because with a finite mind you cannot reach that far with description. Though the terms God and the Father have been used, they are only words to refer to all that is, that has been, that ever will be, from the Isness of what was to the Isness of what is, to the unlimited Isness of forever.

So where do you find a point of reference for becoming God? In you, for what you are is the image of God, the duplicate of what the Father is. The essence that you are is that which is ongoing, evolving, ever-changing, ever-creating, ever-being. You are thought; you are light; you are electrum; you are form. You are pure energy, awesome power, pulsating emotion, sublime thought. That which you have perceived to be the highest level of intelligence — of power, dignity, holiness, and grace — is that which is you. Who are you? You are the identifiable God.

The Father can never be identified outside of your wondrous being. To even attempt it is unfair to yourself because you are going outside of what you are to describe something which emanates from within you. The only way you can identify God is to observe what the Father is in you. And isn't that rather nice, after all? It takes you out of the complexities of trying to comprehend infinite creation and brings you into the here and now of your own life, your own thought processes, your own Isness.

The only way you can perceive, understand, and emotionally know the Father is to understand and emotionally know who you are; then you will know God. Then you can say, "I know who the Father is, for the Father and I are one, and I know who I am."

To be as God is, is to be as you are. When you simply are the Isness of yourself, you are open-ended, unlimited, creative, and optional. You are allowing; you are movement; you are quiet; you are joy. You are pure energy, powerful direction, all feeling, all thought. Being and loving yourself with all of your being and all of your breath and allowing the virtue of yourself into life are being as God is.

Simply allow yourself to be, an Isness. In being, you are everything. To become God is to say, "I am."

**

CHAPTER 11

The Gift Of Love

*The purest form of love is the freedom of will that God gave
each of you so that you would explore the dimensions of
thought and expand the mind of God.*

There is no such thing as the will of God, apart from your
own divine will. If God wanted life to be the mundaneness of a
singular expression, he never would have created you into being,
nor would he have given you the will to express your own
purposeful uniqueness.

What is called the will of God was created by man so that
he could govern and control his brothers. Yet if you believe that
teaching and see God's will as separate from yours, then you will
always be in the battle of his will versus yours, for you will want
to do certain things and feel you must; yet the will of God says
you must not.

God is not separate from you. You and he are one and the
same. Your will is his will. Whatever you want to do is what you
term divine providence, divine will. So you are never in conflict
with destiny, for destiny is not preordained; it is ordained wholly
by you. Everything you think creates your moments to come.
Your very Now moment is simply the product of the thoughts
you had moments ago. That is the science of God. The only
thing the Father wills for you is to experience the totality of life
that he is, according to the feelings within your soul. Why? So
that you come to understand what joy is and the unconditional
love that God has for you and all life.

If you feel you are at odds with God, perhaps you should reconstruct your image of what God is, for I tell you he is not all-loving if you must fight him.

In the beginning when the Father contemplated his most splendid self, he expanded himself into the splendor of light. It was from that expansion in light that each of you became God in the form of a unique, singular movement so that you would continue the expansion of thought into forever.

In order for God to be an ever-expanding uniqueness through your contemplative thoughts, it was necessary to give each of you the power to create uniquely from the thought that he is. And he did this by giving you the action called free will. The principle of will was given to each of you so that you would be unique and sovereign, so that you would be the creator of your own truth, sovereign in your own understanding.

What gives you your divine essence is that you have the freedom to embrace and experience whatever thoughts you desire. And that divine essence, called free will, is love. It is the gift of love from God to each of you. Each of you has the divine essence of will so that you have the freedom to create uniquely whatever ideal you envision through thought.

Love in its ultimate form is the desire of the Father to allow the life that he is to be an ongoingness through each of you. The purest form of love is the freedom of will that the Father gave each of you so that through the exercise of that will, you would explore the dimensions of thought and expand yourself into a greaterness, which expands the mind of God.

Free will gives you a uniqueness — yet a oneness with the Father — that permits your thought processes to have their own creative flow. And every moment you create through the contemplation and expansion of your own thoughts, you imitate the same love that the Father had for himself when he created you into being, for creation is the act of bringing love from within your being into a unique, free-moving, creative form, which will live on into forever.

From the illustrious moment of your birth, the Father gave each of you through pure, unconditional love this covenant:

Whatever you think, whatever you desire, the Father shall become. Through that covenant — that still is and always shall be — each of you became the heir to the totality of what the Father is. Thus the Father always gives you all that he has become so that you can experience and understand the totality of life that he is. He is the basis of the fulfillment of your dreams. But who is the dream-maker? You. And what are your dreams made of? Thought, God, life.

You can take from the totality of thought that God is and create any truth, any attitude, any desire you wish. Whatever truth or attitude you create in your thought processes, the Father, life, readily becomes. And whatever ideal of thought you desire, the Father freely manifests through the matter that he is so that you may experience it.

To give you an example of God's love for you, let us look at the creature called a snake, an ideal created by a God for the purpose of extended life in a life chain. This creature has a long, slender body with many muscles and many bones. It moves very swiftly and has a very big head with fangs that can puncture you as its only defense. Though its bite can bring down a man of great size within moments, any man could hack the snake to bits or easily crush it.

Now let us take two Gods. The first, who has a scientific mind, sees the snake as a wonderful creation, for it can move very swiftly, even without feet, and has a beautiful pattern and color to its skin, and a marvelous skeleton that seems to go on and on and on. The second God comes up and says that the snake is hideous and vile, it is an awful creature because its bite is dangerous, and it can kill a man.

To the Father, the Isness of all life, all things are pure in their state of being. All things are innocent in their expression of the life that he is. It is only each entity's attitude toward something that makes it a beautiful or a vile, ugly thing. It is only we Gods — who have the creative ability to take from the thought that the Father is, contemplate it, and alter it — who judge something that is really pure and innocent as something other than being.

How great is the love of God — which is the life substance that the snake is — that he gives you, his greatest creation, the right to cast your attitude and will upon the snake however you choose? The love that the life source has for you is so great that it will become any one thing that you desire through thought. The Father will be anything you wish him to be. He will allow you to alter him in any way you wish to alter him. The life that he is will become vile or ugly or vulgar, or it will become to the height of beauty; however you wish to see it.

Now is that not a wondrous thing, that the Father will become however you perceive and desire him to be simply through the whims of your thought processes? Indeed it is. That is love.

You can do with thought whatever you will, for the Father's love for you is steadfast. No matter how vile or wretched you perceive the life that God is, to him it is still him. It is still God. It is still pure, and it is still loved. That promise is unshakable, for the Father is of himself wholly without attitudes; he simply is.

The love between you and God has no condition. If the Father in any way censored your thoughts or restricted you from experiencing the totality of the life that he is, then you would not have the freedom to continue his expansion into forever. Neither would you gain the wisdom from your adventures in thought in order to understand the love and joy that the Father truly is in his supreme state of being.

God loves you in complete freedom to do as you will, for your will is his will. That is the covenant between God and his sons, God and himself. Whatever you do, wherever you venture unto him, you are always loved. He allows you to do whatever you desire, for he knows that you are ongoing, that nothing can ever take you from him. The Father has created no thing superior to himself that can remove your life force ever, so you will always be. And when your life here is spent, there will be yet another, with the freedom to create it however you choose.

You will live this life and all of those to come according to your will. And what has given you the freedom to do that is that which loves you, that which is called your Father, God Almighty, the lover of all things.

You are free entities. How? Through the power called will and the ability called love.

CHAPTER 12

Nothing But Truth

Do you know what the truth is? That there is none. There being none means that everything is.

Student: I feel like I've spent my whole life going from one religion to another and, more recently, from one teacher to another trying to understand what life and God are all about. I'm really confused, Ramtha, because everyone has something different to say. Even though many things are the same, they all teach different things, and some of them are even completely the opposite of the other.

For instance, you say that there is no right or wrong and that God loves us whatever we do. In a way, what you teach makes sense to me, but it's very different than what others teach. And some of what you teach seems a little far-out in a sense because it's so different than what I have been taught my whole life.

I'm confused, Ramtha. I don't know who to believe. How do I determine what is really true, what the truth is?

Ramtha: First, master, what mean you by the term far-out?

Student: Well, what I mean is, one has to stretch his thoughts to understand or accept some of the things you say.

Ramtha: Would you say that infinity and forever are far-out?

Student: Well, yes, in a way.

Ramtha: Then my teachings are indeed far-out, for that is how far they will take you, all the way to the perimeters of forever.

Now tell me, master, what is not true?

Student: Well, for example, imagination, fantasy, things that don't correspond with reality.

Ramtha: Indeed? What are imagination and fantasy?

Student: Thoughts you entertain in your mind; things you make up in your thoughts.

Ramtha: And when you are entertaining these thoughts, are they not real? Are they not a reality in your consciousness? Are they not a truth in thought?

Student: Yes, but they may be true only in my mind. They don't necessarily correspond with the truth about how things really are in reality.

Ramtha: You know, master, everyone wishes to know what the truth is. But if there is the truth, what is everything other than that when it also has a reality in consciousness?

Do you know what the truth is? That there is none. There being none means that everything is.

Everything is true, master. There is nothing untrue, for all things are derived from thought, which is God. And God is not one formulated thought; he is the reality of all thoughts.

Everything is real, for everything has been given credence through thought and has purpose in being. What you term imagination and fantasy are certainly real, for they are constituted of purposeful thought.

Student: Even though they don't correspond with the real world that is out there?

Ramtha: The world out there, which you call real, master, is only the illusion and creation of the greatest reality of all, which is the unseen reality called thought and emotion. How do you think all of your world out there came into being? It was created by imagination and fantasy. And once it became a reality in its material form, it then spurred further imagination and fantasy, for each begets the other and both are indeed real.

Everything created in thought, everything that exists in consciousness — whether or not it is ever manifested into the form called material reality — is true, master.

Student: No matter how bizarre it is?

Ramtha: Indeed, entity, for only attitudes determine bizarreness. Every thought entertained in your mind is true, for it is alive in consciousness; thus it is a part of the greatest reality, termed the mind of God, the platform from which all life springs forth.

Now let us see, master, if we can help you out a bit with your confusion. God the Father is thought, the truth of all thought. And the splendid thing about God is that he is indeed lawless, for if the Father had laws, he would be limited. But since the Father is unlimited, he allows options to his unlimited truth, unlimited thought. The Father has given each of you the will to accept and create from thought whatever truth adds to your own individuality, to perceive truth according to your desire and your unique progression into wisdom. And whatever truth you create in thought, the Father, life, will become so you may experience and understand that truth, that dimension of thought called God.

Truth is only what an individual perceives truth to be. Truth is an opinion, an attitude, a belief about something that has become an absolute in creative thought. Yet everyone's opinion about any one thing will differ often vastly, for each has formulated that opinion based on his unique experiences and the understanding or misunderstanding that he has gained in his soul, not only from this life but from all lives lived before this one. So one entity will believe something to be true and another may not. The two cannot comprehend one another because they have not been one another and had the same collective experiences.

Whose truth is correct? Both are. They are both truthfully right, for each is expressing the truth which his experience and understanding have allowed him to perceive. But if one's truth is that his truth is the only one that is correct, he is limited in his understanding.

Each entity in this dream — according to his experience and his own need and for the purpose of the fulfillment of self — will accept and create whatever truths he desires to experience for his evolution into wisdom. And for the purpose of that experience, each will seek out sources of truth which support what he wants to believe. Thus for however many Gods that inhabit this plane, there will be that many unique sets of truths, for each entity has the will and the right and the need to create truth differently.

So whatever you read or hear from a teacher is perceived truth: how he sees it, how he has learned it, how he has created it, how he is experiencing it. Thus if you studied under ten teachers, you would certainly be in great confusion, for each one's truth will be different. And you may certainly find that one or another's perception of truth will fit whatever you are needing at the moment. But if you are trying to discern which one speaks the truth when you look at all of them, you will realize that all of them do. What you must decide is to what degree you wish to become a particular truth, for whatever truth you accept will become an experienced reality in your life.

There are great teachers on your plane, master, and they are magicians of sorts, for they can do and manifest wondrous and miraculous things. But they still believe in death, and thus they will die. Even though they have progressed greatly in their learning, they have not yet taken their understanding beyond the limitations of death and dying to the understanding that life is really a continuum in being. So if you were to accept their truths as the truth, you too might become a magician, but you will also die. You see?

There is truth in everything, master, but there is also refinement in all things, for each moment refines truth. That is why God is not in a state of perfection but rather a state of becoming. Each entity continually progresses in his understanding to encompass more unlimited truth. And whatever his understanding is, moment to moment to moment, it will be the truth as he sees it, as he knows it.

Let us take a flower, for example. Is it true that the flower is a bud? Indeed. When the flower blooms, is it a liar because it is no longer a bud? No. It is in a state of progressive truth. And is the flower a liar when its petals fall and are no more? What is it then? It is in a further state of its truth.

Any teachings that you hear or read from a source that teaches of laws — or limits man, or divides the Isness into good and evil, or says that God is a singular entity rather than the Isness of all that is — any teachings like that are coming from entities who simply have accepted that to be their truth and are compelled to give it to the world. That is their truth, master, and they are not wrong. But a greater, more refined truth is that anyone who teaches that life is in any way limited has not progressed in his understanding as greatly as others have. For is God limited? If he were, master, life would not be ongoing and you would not even have the option to be confused.

What I teach is indeed a wondrous truth, for who dares to call God lawless, for then he cannot be used to control and enslave others. But the Father, the supreme consciousness, is indeed without the limitation of laws and judgments and endings. When you progress in your truth to embrace that unlimited understanding, then you will experience and truly understand the love and joy and ongoingness that the Father is.

Everyone knows, master, only to the extent that they desire and allow themselves to know. And most knowledge on your plane is built upon fear and survival and polarities of understanding. It is built upon judgment and the separation of peoples. It is built upon the understanding that man is a fallen creature who has no divinity. But man is God, master; thus to judge man is to judge God. To limit man is to limit God. To separate man from his divinity is to take divinity away from God.

If what you read or hear from a teacher limits your thought processes, it indeed limits the thought processes of the Father. Listen to what is said and how it is said. If it limits, separates, divides, then it is a limiting truth of an entity who has yet to progress into a more unlimited understanding.

What you inevitably learn from all of these teachers, master, is that you alone are your greatest teacher, for only you know what is the best of all things for you. How can anyone else know when he is busy living his own life and assessing truth from his own point of view? Only you can know what experience is needed in your soul for your own fulfillment. Only you can be the giver of your own truth, for truth is self-ordained and self-established. And that truth will not be found through scientific or intellectual understandings but rather through an emotional understanding, for truth is a feeling, a knowingness; it is not intellectual. To know what the truth is for you is to know what you feel the truth is.

Student: But, Ramtha, how can you feel that something is true if it is not supported by facts, or if it is perhaps contrary to what science has discovered to be true?

Ramtha: Master, nothing can be proven by what you term facts, for facts will change as the understanding of mankind evolves and changes. Everything is conjecture, for reality is continually evolved and created through thought and emotion. Facts are only the current material manifestations of collective consciousness, collective thoughts that have been embraced into emotion by the whole of mankind.

The proof, master, is in the feeling, in emotion, for that is what gave reality to the fact in the first place.

What is the greatest reality, the greatest truth? Not facts, master. It is the feelings you have by accepting facts as reality, as truths in thought. That is the true fact. It is emotion that is the greatest reality. That is where all truth lies.

Whatever you choose to believe, master, so it will be. So now you choose what is proper for you, what you wish to believe.

Student: But, Ramtha, I don't understand how that could be. For example, in times when most people believed the earth was flat, if half of the sailors on a boat thought that the earth was round and half thought that it was flat and they sailed off to sea, what happened to the boat?

Ramtha: Those who thought it was flat, master, flung themselves overboard. Heaven forbid they should be proven wrong. The ones who thought it was round continued the journey. You see?

Those who believed firmly that the world was flat never ventured to the edge to find out differently, for they were sure it was flat. Those who believed it was round sailed around and around and around. And they were convinced that it was round. But they did not know that it is not round. It is rather squashed. It is bursting at its seams, flat-headed and flat-bottomed, and it is hollow. But those who firmly believe it is solid will never know otherwise, for they will never contemplate going inward to find out differently. That is because they are of a limited understanding, which nonetheless is still true.

Be unlimited in your truth, master. Know that your world is round. But if you wish to be even more unlimited in your truth, know that it is flattened on its top and bottom. And to be even more unlimited, know that it is hollowed. And to be even more unlimited than that, entity, know that the center of your earth is very much inhabited. But try to tell your scientists that.

If what you believe is of a limited form, then that is your truth, and you are correct and precise. If you believe in an unlimited form, then that is your truth, correct and precise. But if you are searching for something to believe in, don't believe in either. Believe in you. There is no entity, no thing, no reality that is greater than you are, for you are the giver of all truth, the creator of all realities, the dispenser of all laws within your kingdom.

Now what I would tell any one entity is this: Go and learn from your teachers or your religions until you are bored or it makes no more sense. Then seek the answer that feels right within your soul. Your soul knows what the truth is, and it will tell you through feelings. When the truth feels right, that is your soul rejoicing, because the grandest truth is unlimited freedom, whatever allows you to experience any truth you desire.

Truth is a limitation, master. To say that anything is true indicates there is untruth. But in a greater understanding there is neither truth nor untruth; there is only the Isness of ongoing, evolving life. Life is the only reality and from that all truth emerges, for truth is evolved and created every moment by every thought you have. Thus in any moment you can change your mind and think something else, and yet they are both true. They are both real principles, for both are options for emotional understanding.

There is no reality but life and options. When you understand that everything is true and nothing is — that there is only Isness — then you can perceive truth to be whatever you determine it to be, and it will be absolute as long as you recognize it as such. The moment you don't recognize and give credence to that truth, it is no longer real. That is why this plane is the plane of creative realities.

Whatever truth you create in your life, know that you also can change. What allows you to become sovereign is to know that you can do and become anything you want and that you have the ability to change your mind anytime you want.

How long does it take you to become happy? Only long enough for you to think joy, and you will begin to beam. How long does it take you to become despairing? As long as it takes you to think despair, and you will become it. What is the underlying truth in this? That you have the option to become either anytime you desire, and that you can change your expression anytime you desire. That is the freedom the Father loves you with. When you know that truth within your being, you will exceed your limitedness into your godhood. And when others have permitted themselves to be governed with laws and morals and ideals, you will be a free entity, for you will belong to no truth but your own.

Only remember this: Whatever you think to be, is. Anytime you believe in anything, it becomes truth in an emotional reality within your being. That is why everyone is always on the pinnacle of truth, no matter what that point of view is. Your creative reality will always be different from everyone else's. And when others utterly fail to see your reality, it is only because they are so immersed in the illusions of their own.

When you understand that truth is and can be all things, then you have not limited yourself from experiencing all things. Then you can readily participate in all experiences and have knowledge of them. Then you are free, for you are no longer enslaved to concepts or intellectual understandings that say this is how it is, when how it is, is truly everything that can be defined in thought.

This truth I give you, master, provides a greater unlimitedness in being, for in its virtue and context it embraces everyone else's truth and allows all truths to coexist in harmony. When you embrace this understanding, then you can say to yourself, "Of the truth that I express, I am multifaceted in my truth. I am not one truth but all truth." Then you are no longer inhibited in your creative flow or cloistered into one form of living and being.

Be who you are, not under the direction of Ramtha or Buddha or Yeshua or any other teacher, for none can teach you of your God-self; they can teach you only of theirs. To fulfill your destiny, you must become who and what you uniquely are. If you try to live according to another's life plan, you will never become that. The only way you will come to understand who you are and this fire that lives within you is through the truth of your own emotional understanding.

Love what you are intently and listen to the God within you, which speaks a very subtle tone. It is called feelings. The feelings, if you listen to them, will tell you of truth and your path for enlightenment.

Live the truth you feel inside you. Live it and manifest it so that it attests to the glory of you. When you do, then you will have assessed, lived, and understood life from your point of view. And however you perceive it, it will all be right. Be your own teacher, your own savior, your own master, your own God.

When you contemplate the simplicity of this, it will release you into the freedom to understand. Then you will not get caught up in trying to determine what is true and what is not, what is real and what is illusion. When you begin to remove yourself from the laws of religious dogma and belief and cease striving to be another's truth, then you are free to express yourself and experience the things that your soul calls you to do, so you can be fulfilled in whatever knowledge and understanding you are lacking. Then through experience and emotion, you at your own individualized pace become God, moment by moment by moment. And where shall your eternity end? Nowhere, for you are ongoing into forever.

When you learn that each moment you live, you are refining your own opinionated self — and when you allow yourself to do that without guilt and judgment of self — then one day you become the truth of all thought, the platform from which all life springs forth. But you cannot become that until you remove yourself from the collective consciousness of man — with its laws, ideals, and mass identity — and allow yourself to be the Isness of your own truth, of your own purposeful self.

For a long time man has separated himself from his divinity by taking away all of his options and creating laws in place of them. But the winds of change are upon this plane to bring about a newness, a reckoning in everyone, an unsettling of what has been considered absolute. I am pleased you have come to be a part of it, for your life will be much more joyous from this day forth. For who are you to answer to? No one but yourself. And what is the truth? Whatever self decrees it to be, for whatever you believe, so it is; and whatever you believe, so you will become. Know that, and you will teach many just by the way you live.

Never seek truth. Simply be. In being, you are at one with infinite universes.

Student: There's much for me to contemplate.

Ramtha: Indeed, master. Isness. So be it.

Student: I have been practicing astrology for several years now, and I want to know if there is something you can tell me which will help me to be more effective with my clients.

Ramtha: First, master, tell me why you delight yourself in this practice.

Student: Because I believe that the stars and planets have an influence on our lives and that by studying them, we can better know and understand ourselves and our destiny.

Ramtha: You know, master, man has always gazed at the silent mystery of the stars in your heavens in search for his homeland, for he knows instinctively within him that he came from a far greater place than the hovel where he was born. When man began to search the lights in the sky at night, he noticed to his amazement that they moved. And as they moved, the seasons moved with them. And when he observed a power in them that he could not control, he reckoned that their movements must also be responsible for the fortunes and misfortunes that befall the kingdom of man.

There has been many a wise man, prophet, or sage who

has used the powerful belief in the stars to govern and rule empires. And if their prophecies of peril came true, who was responsible? Certainly not the seer. Then it must be the damnable stars that caused it to be so. Yet the stars, in their silence, have never been able to defend themselves and proclaim their innocence.

I will tell you this, master. Everyone here is a God who was created with free will. And in your beginning, you, the lightbeings, as sovereign entities, used that freedom of will to create the stars, the planets, and all the universes, seen and unseen. You are also the Gods who would later create the embodiments that you possess, which are far greater than any universe. You are this very moment the same Gods who still possess the same powerful creativeness that you had in your beginning. And in all of those eons of time you have never created anything to control you, unless you believe that it does. And in that you are still the controller of your life, for you have accepted the belief that you are controlled by something outside of your being; thus you have allowed it to be so.

There are many who believe in astrology. And it does indeed have its truth, for it is believed to be a truth. But take it a step further and ask who the giver of this truth is and how the stars and planets in their movements could be greater than the Gods who created them in the first place.

Who you are, master, will never be discovered through the movement in your heavens. And regarding the movement of the planets and the stars determining one's destiny, 'tis not so, for if that were a truth, we would not have such things as dreams, or imagination, or creativity, or life.

In each of your lives upon this plane you were born under many stars, all of which were shining at that time. To say that your destiny is controlled or influenced by a select few is not only unreasonable, master, but it takes away your freedom and innocence to express your life and the God that you are.

The Gods have created many games, and astrology is one of them. And at times it is a very dangerous game because it instills in the entity a fear of his future and predetermines his future days of emotion. Those who think that astrologers possess all-wise, knowing intelligence are literally putting forth their valuable lives into the hands of another, and I am not in agreement with that.

As your astrology is a game, so is your religious dogma, so is your politics, so is your marketplace, so is everything that you allow to enslave you so that you can play the game of survival.

Those who practice astrology are indeed beautiful in their true concern for others and their desire to help them. And to study the stars is a wonderful thing, for they are beautiful in their movement and enchanting in their mystery. But if you base your life upon them, master, you are no greater than the gases that make them up.

Astrology is only a tool; it is only a game. The real truth is coming through the entity who is opening his mouth to say, "Alas, I have determined what your future will bring," because he has picked up on the emotional, magnetic, electrical field surrounding the entity for whom he is doing this. If you were to remove the game and tell the client these same things, it would certainly be amazing to him. But of course it would not be nearly as intriguing as saying that a certain star is at fault and that he is a part of some divine, cosmic plan. So it was with the wise men of old who looked into crystal balls, lit fires, gazed upon water, made explosions, drank wine and elixirs and all sorts of things, only to convey a truth by making it more acceptable.

Man has always looked outside of himself to find answers and reasons for his fate and his destiny. It has always been more comforting to blame the silent stars or the rule of kings or the will of God than to look within to the creator of the universes. It has always been easier to seek out priests and prophets and seers for guidance than to believe that oneself is wise enough to be the giver of it.

As long as you look outside of yourself for reasons and answers, you will never hear the voice within you, the giver of all truth and the creator of all that is. You will always be at the hands of superstitious beliefs and outrageous reasonings that blind you to the awesome power and infinite understanding that you truly possess.

You, master, are a sovereign entity who can accept and create any truth you want. You can become the master of your kingdom or allow yourself to be the slave, whichever you desire to experience. When you realize that each entity is the true creator and controller of his life, the designer of his destiny, perhaps you will take that same realization and create for yourself a more unlimited life. And that will be a very grand thing for your being.

When you are playing with your games, remember who created them. And remember that the same creator, who can become vulnerable to anything he wishes to, can in a moment change whatever he does not like and once again take hold of his life.

Now I wish to tell you this in regard to the game of astrology. Astrologers are basing their houses on twelve, yet there are fourteen. There is a planet that is considered to be a star but is rather a nebula. It is a beautiful, luminous planet that has been here for a very long time. That is another house, as it were. And already in the cradle orbit of your sun there is a new planet formulating, which was brought forth several thousand years ago when the sun's flares were great. That, master, is fourteen. How can astrologers be so accurate when they are off by two whole houses?

When you do these readings, master, I desire for you to do this: After you have plotted and planned and all of that, when the reading is finished, tell them that the universes are nothing without them; that without them, there would not have been any such things as stars or planets. That is all you have to say. They will never forget what you have said, for it will bother them. It will uplift them, and it will make them arrogant.

I am pleased you have come here. You will learn profoundly from this audience. Of those who come here, there are many who will not embrace the unlimited truths that I teach, for not all are desirous of freedom. But that is all right. They are still loved, and they are still right, and they are still God, the creator of all realities.

***

CHAPTER 13

The Lawlessness Of Life

When man frees himself from this restrictive consciousness with its laws and plans and rules, he will find the joy and peace of being that will allow him to love himself and all mankind.

Student: Ramtha, how do you fit into God's plan?

Ramtha: God's plan? What makes you think, entity, that God has a plan?

Student: Because there must be a good reason why things are the way they are.

Ramtha: The only plan that the Father has is to be, so that everything can express the life that the Father is. If he had a plan, as it were, it would take away your freedom to express the God within you, which would take away your uniqueness and your ability to evolve yourself and expand the life principle called God.

God's only plan is that it is. It is everything vibrating at one with itself, at a tone that is based first in thought, and from thought into mass — vibrating, adding and taking from consciousness, elongating — expressing yet another moment of life. Everything that is, expresses abreast of everything else that is, into the next moment of eternity. If God could plan, it would limit everything that is to come.

This hairy rug that you have your rump upon, what is the reason it is here? Simply because it is. Thus it fits into God's plan because everything else is. And what is the reason this beloved master is here? Because he is. And this beloved master, how does he fit into God's plan? By simply being, just as you are being. And how do I fit in? I am, entity. I am, as much as this hairy rug is.

How do I fit in? I will love you as grandly as anyone will ever love you because I have the capacity to do that, for I do not worry about whether my love or expression fits in with some illusive, divine plan.

How do I add to the overall Isness of life? By helping you understand what the Father truly is and why it loves you — regardless of however you are — and by bringing perhaps into a clearer focus how all of life fits together so you may understand that the reason everything is, is simply to express not according to any scheme, not for any ulterior motive, but simply because it has life.

Why is that important? When you understand that life simply is, that allows you the freedom and the power to create your life to the greatest of your ability. And you may rest assured that whatever you do in the next moment, you will be vibrating amongst all life, and you will continue to do so in the next moment and the next one and the ones to come thereafter.

There is not a plan for life, master. There is only Isness. To be in a state of Isness is the grandest expression there is — Isness. What matters, entity, is that you are. That is all that matters.

Student: What you seem to be saying is that there is no particular way that one should live; that you can be and do anything you want; that anything goes.

Ramtha: Indeed. That is the love of the Father for you.

Student: Well, what then is the purpose of life?

Ramtha: The purpose of life, master, is to express upon the platform of life whatever thoughts you entertain within your being. And whatever expression that leads you to, know that you always have the option to change it at any moment you desire.

The purpose of life is to be a part of it, to be the creator of it, to illuminate it. There is no other destiny than to live and to allow yourself to be whatever you desire to be as life unfolds within you, moment to moment to moment. And in fulfilling that purpose, know that you have the unlimited freedom to become and do and be whatever you desire.

Student: But if you can do anything, won't certain things go against the law of God that is spoken of in the Bible?

Ramtha: My beautiful master, your beloved Father has created no law, save one, and that law is to express your life according to your own sovereign will, for only through the exercise of your will do you expand the consciousness of all life, which is what the Father is. If God the Father were a law-creating entity, he would have denied you — himself — the freedom of expression that allows life to evolve and perpetuate itself. He would have become a limited source, an ending. There is no ending to forever, master.

What you term the law of God, as it is written in your Book of Books, is many laws, for each prophet added to the law. It has indeed been a powerful statement to say that the law of God says this or that, or it restricts this, or you must do that. And because of what you term the law of God, people have learned to surrender to God and to fear him. Children are not to fear their parents; they are to be as their parents.

The law of one is that God, the Source of all life, allows all things to express through his being as they will, as their freedom desires, for it is only through freedom that you will come to know the Father and be one with him once again. And when you return to the Father and he contemplates the homecoming of himself, it will be a great day indeed, a great forever, for in your coming home you will have come to be as he is. And in being as he is, is there always a life of unlimited love, unlimited joy, and the foreverness of being.

God the Father is lawless. Man is the law creator, not God. The Father has given man the freedom of will to be the sovereign lawgiver of his own kingdom, to create from thought whatever belief, truth, or attitude befits his kingdom in his evolving understanding of all life. Man has used that freedom to create laws that are deemed necessary in order to live in society. Unfortunately, most laws have been created ruthlessly for the purpose of intimidating and enslaving people. They have been created to limit freedom, not to exalt it. Man cannot permit himself to be in a lawless state because he, in the terror of his own being, thinks there must be laws to govern his being. That is only because he does not understand the infiniteness and divineness of himself.

Student: But, Ramtha, if there were no laws, how could you prevent someone from expressing the evil within him, from doing bad things?

Ramtha: Let me tell you this, master. In the cosmic makeup of all that is, there is no such thing as evil. Though it has been written that man is evil in his soul, he is not. He is divine in his soul, for his soul and all that he is, is God, because if it is not God, then where did it come from?

There is nothing outside of the jurisdiction of the Father, of beingness. Nothing. Any thought or deed that anyone has judged to be evil or bad or wrong is alive in consciousness. And if it exists in consciousness, it is certainly a part of the mind of God. And since everything is a part of God, if you were to say that any one thing is evil, you would also be saying that God is evil, and he is not. Neither is God good, for in order to define the perimeters of good, it must be weighed against the understanding called bad or evil.

God is neither good nor bad, for God is not a good thing any more than an evil thing. Neither is God perfection. The Father simply is, the Isness of all life, a Now expression that lives simply for the joy of obtaining joy in order to know itself. And that life essence does not have the capacity to alter itself out of a state of Isness by judging a part of itself as being good or bad, evil or divine, perfect or imperfect.

Do you know what would happen if God could look down and say this is evil? The whole of that consciousness that is expressing something it needs to express would be terminated from the life force. And if that could happen, then life and its ongoing expansion would cease to exist, for free will, which allows creation, would cease to exist. But God is wholly unlimited, an undivided totality of Isness. Thus God cannot peer at itself in a limited, restrictive view. If it could, you would not even be here to express your option to judge yourself or your brothers.

There is neither good nor bad, master; there is only Isness. In the Isness, all things are measured solely in terms of fulfillment, in terms of the emotional experience needed by the soul to fulfill itself in wisdom. Everything that you have ever done — however beautiful or vile you have determined it to be — you have done simply for the sake of knowing. You were pressed by your soul and your passions to do it in order to learn. Only by doing it did you realize and ascertain the value of that doing and thus gain from it. That is neither evil nor is it wicked; that is what it takes to become God.

Man — not God — judges man. And man in his creativity has devised the balance of good and evil to take from his brothers their freedom of expression. The fear of punishment for not being in line with religious dogma or the laws of governments has been the sword that has ruled and controlled nations for ages. And if ever there were what you call in your terms an evil thing, it is that which takes away the freedom of an entity to express the God within him. And each time that is done to another, it is also being done to self and more profoundly so, for whatever judgment or limitation you place upon another, it becomes a law within your own consciousness. And by that law so shall you be limited and so shall you judge yourself.

Man is not evil in his soul. Though he lives under the auspices of it, in a greater understanding there is no such thing as evil. There is only the platform of life that allows man the option to create from his thinking whatever he chooses. That is the only reality there is. In that reality, God allows the illusion of evil to be created through superstition, dogmatic beliefs, and the very limited, cloistered attitudes of mankind. And through the continuous observation, judgment, and expectancy of evil, it does indeed exist in one's reality but only in his reality, for as he believes, so his kingdom is.

The only laws that exist are those that you create to be effective in your life. If you choose to believe there is good and evil, then that is your truth, and you are not wrong at all. But, remember, it is your truth; not mine or anyone else's. And if indeed it is yours, it collectively belongs to you because it is formed in your opinion. As long as you have that opinion, it will certainly be real. When you no longer believe it, it will no longer be a reality. That is simply how it is.

Now, master, do tell me what you think evil is. What is your understanding of bad?

Student: Well, I would say that it's the opposite of good. But mostly what I think evil is, is harming another person.

Ramtha: Indeed? Why is that evil?

Student: Well, for example, if someone harmed my daughter, it's evil because, let's say, she might die.

Ramtha: That is your judgment of evil. But what is evil about dying?

Student: So you don't even think that killing someone is evil?

Ramtha: That is correct, because I have not limited myself by believing in the ending of any one thing, for nothing is ever destroyed — ever. So if an entity dies, what is the loss in death?

The Father, in his Isness and eternalness of ongoing life, has not created any one thing greater than himself that could disturb the guarantee of all existence. What the Father created, master, nothing can put under; it will eternally live. So your child would not have been destroyed, because nothing can destroy the life of God.

Student: So you're saying that even murder is not wrong or evil.

Ramtha: That is correct.

I tell you, master, life is ongoing. It will go on and on and on. And moment into moment into moment, as we express upon the platform of life, we have unlimited opportunities to fulfill ourselves in happiness in each moment of life. But however one chooses to fulfill his moments, it will always be according to his will and his desire and what he perceives to be good for his being. And if in the moment an entity chooses to slay another, then in the next moment he will live in awesome guilt and self-judgment and the fear that somehow that act will come back to him. Thus his moments to come are not secure unless he forgives himself for the act.

There are many who will be horrified and who will judge

and curse the slayer. But I love the entity that has slain the other, for how can I not? Is he outside of the providence and the life and the wonderment of God? Nay, he is not, master.

The slain will come back again and again, for life is perpetual. It is continuous. It is the only thing that is perpetual, yet it is all things. If I abhor the act and place judgment upon the slayer, I have placed it upon myself. The slayer has already created his own judgment, for he will be at the hands of whatever attitudes he has regarding the act, which he will have to deal with in his own kingdom of thought and emotion in the moments that follow.

I do not abhor the act. I have reasoned it. I have understood it. I am beyond it. If I judge the slayer for that act, I am no grander for it, I assure you, and my life will then be affected by that judgment, for the I Am that I am will have taken a part of itself and separated it from my being. Then I am no longer whole. You see?

When you see such things, they are fulfillments occurring. In each moment we have the option to fulfill ourselves in a way that we feel driven to or that we feel enlightened to. That is our choice. That is the only republic man has, the republic deep within himself. Your governments will try to govern the mass according to laws and rules and regulations, but they will never govern the will of an entity that works in the silence of his own thought processes. Only the entity can do that. And each moment he lives, he balances the moment according to his own emotional being.

I say in this audience that there is no grander teacher than you are and that each is wholly responsible for his own life's accord, for are we not the ones who in thought do one thing, and is it not the manifestation of that one thing that will teach our thoughts to be more refined?

You can take a man and put him in prison — into the smallest, darkest, filthiest pit there is — but you will never imprison his mind and his thinking. A man with his body stifled is still active in thought. And he, through contemplative thought, will reason with himself and teach himself and judge himself.

I do not acknowledge good or evil, only life. If it moves

an entity to slay another — or to do it within his soul by simply thinking about it — one is not greater than the other, for what you have done in your thoughts, you have already done. And there is not one entity that has not cleaved another in his thoughts. That entity in either case needs to express that for his purposeful understanding. And I wish you to understand that one who participates with the slayer in his expression is not the victim of the slayer, for he has contemplated the possibility of perhaps being burned, or cleaved in two, or molested. And because he had contemplated it and it is fearsome, he has drawn it right to his doorstep. Thus the one who needs to molest and the one who needs to be molested — because he needs to understand it — are brought together for the experience.

In the understanding called God, nothing is evil. Everything is an experience that provides wisdom. That is my answer to you. And when man is no longer condemned by his brothers and realizes that he is not evil in his being — that he is God in his being — and understands that he is wholly loved and supported by the life force called God, he will no longer need to experience war or rape or murder, or other such acts, in order to understand his worth and value. And when man frees himself from this restrictive consciousness, with its laws and plans and rules, he will find the joy and peace of being that will allow him to love himself and the whole of mankind and allow all to be in the freedom of their own willful designs. Then he will love as God loves. Then he will be as God is, the platform which nurtures and supports all life. So be it.

Student: There are two people who have come into my life recently, and I want to know what their purpose is in my life and whether we have been together before in other lives.

Ramtha: The reason they are in your life, entity, is because you want them there and they want to be there. What greater purpose can there be than that?

Student: But I am not sure whether I want them in my life. I thought maybe they were there because of some karmic tie we had with each other and that there was something we needed to learn from each other.

Ramtha: You know, master, if a relationship is somewhat lacking, the romanticism of perhaps having been together before in past lives often makes it so much more glamorous than it is now. But a karmic tie, as it is termed, is only a religious explanation of a very simple word called need. You will need and enjoy and want to be with many people throughout all of your lives, which are continuous. But it would become very mundane, very dull and boring, if the same friends were there life after life after life. If they are there now, perhaps the only lesson to be associated with it, master, is that you have come together once again only to realize you need to go apart again.

Student: Okay. I think I understand what you are saying, but I have another question about karma. I've been taught that the reason things happen to people — things like murders or robberies or accidents — is because they are karmic fulfillments to balance something they did in a past life. I would like to know what you have to say about the laws of karma.

Ramtha: For you to know and for all to understand, what you term karma is not the law of God; it is the law of those who believe in it. Unfortunately, there are multitudes who believe in this doctrine, and they are struggling arduously to attain an illusionary understanding called perfection. And they believe that whatever they do in life, they must come back and pay for in the next one. Everything that happens to them they continuously attribute to karmic fulfillment. But that is a very poor explanation for life, master. It deserves much more than that.

The laws of karma are indeed a reality but only for those who believe in them. The only laws that exist are those which you allow to be effective in your kingdom. The true lawgiver is each sovereign entity, for each possesses an ego that accepts truth. And whatever he calls truth, whatever he creates as a law in his being, so it will be. Thus it is through belief and altered understanding that many have set up for themselves the laws of balance and perfection.

If you choose to believe in karma, you will certainly be at the hands of your own creation, for you have given power to that belief. Then of course it will be effective in your life. Then you will certainly return again and again to nullify or glorify what you did in a previous life upon this plane.

I do not recognize karma or perfection, for I see them as limitations, not gratifications. Those who are struggling for perfection through the restrictiveness of karma will never achieve what they are struggling for, for as they are fulfilling one karma, they would be creating yet another. And no matter how many lifetimes they live, they will never reach a state of Isness, a state of God, for they will be continuously immersed in indebtedness rather than receivership. And there is no such thing as perfection; there is only Isness. In the Isness of life, everything changes and evolves every moment; thus a state of perfection can never be established.

I recognize only Isness, which is wholly without laws and ideals that inhibit the becoming of self, God. In the understanding of Isness, there is nothing you must do in life except what you want to do. If you want to accept the teachings of karma, then that is your choice and your creation for your experience. But realize, master, that you have created for yourself the illusions of limited power and retribution. That is your lot through the acceptance of what is called karma, to be a prisoner of your own limited thinking.

You are a free soul and Spirit, master. You are free to create and experience in the moment whatever truth, whatever reality, whatever illusion you so choose. And in any moment you wish, you can re-create this dream, for you have the unlimited power to do so.

Karma does not exist; want does. And want is very fickle. It can do and be anything at any moment it wishes, and it can change its mind in the midst of being it.

Such things as murders, accidents, and robberies are not punishments, master; they are not repays for what you did before. They are created by you as a result of contemplated thoughts, contemplated experiences. Nor are they forever things, forever circumstances. So in a greater understanding, they are not terrible things. In retrospect, they are great teachers.

You may see the slaughter of ten thousand innocents, and

you may say, "Woe unto such a misery. Why don't the angels weep for this atrocity? Why do they sing to the glory of God?" Because they have not limited themselves by believing that life ever ends. They know that those who are slaughtered are immediately caught up into heaven, as you term it, for a greater learning and more experiences and what I call adventures. And though you bury ten thousand bodies and you weep over them, God does not weep. That is why tomorrow always comes.

Who do you think creates your destiny? Many believe it to be a sovereign who manipulates everyone and causes all things to happen, because that takes the responsibility for their own lives off their backs. But you control your own destiny. You are the creator of every moment of your life by what you think and feel in this moment. You only have to learn that this moment, this Now, is indeed forever, 'tis ongoing. And in the ongoingness of this Now, each moment is brand new. It is brand new, master. It is not the captive of yesterday. It is the Now that you created to dream tomorrow into reality; thus you are free to do anything you wish to do in this moment. That is the Father's love for you: the freedom and the power that he has given you to create each moment anew.

No one is ruled by the past. Whatsoever you did a moment ago or a millennium ago, you do not have to pay for anytime. The very moment you did it, you gained understanding and realized the purposeful good from doing it.

The past was simply a Now moment that was experienced and is no more. The only bearing it has on the present is that you already learned all you could learn from it. Thus it has provided you the wisdom to create this moment to the grandest of your ability, according to your own intimate thought processes and purposeful designs.

The past is finished, master; it is no more. The past lives within you in this Now only as wisdom. That is what it has gained you. That is why in this Now you are the greatest you have ever been in all your lives, for in this Now you have progressed into knowingness further than your yester-Now. You are this moment the cumulative whole of all your knowledge — knowledge gained through experience — and experience gained through the virtue called life. And every moment you express, you are creating anew a new adventure into emotion and the pearls of experience called wisdom.

There is only the Isness of this Now, master. What is important is now. You are the product of Now. Your life is lived in the Now. Your future is created in the Now. To truly live as an Isness in this Now is to live without laws and rules and regulations that inhibit the expression and expansion of self. When you live as an Isness, the only thing that ever matters is now — not the past, not the future, but now — for that is precisely where God lives.

When you realize that now is all there ever is, you will inevitably choose to live your life in such a way that in each moment you live the adventure that the feelings in your soul urge you to pursue, that you are experiencing whatever you have never experienced before in order to expand yourself into even greater wisdom.

You have not come back to this plane to work out certain things, which you cannot even remember, or to do certain things that you are supposed to do, which no one can ever tell you what they are. And yet you are told to strive for perfection. How can you ever achieve anything if you are continuously in confusion?

You have come back here wholly by choice through a body that you chose. From the egg of your mother and the sperm of your father, you created your body for the purpose of expressing on this plane of creative illusion. You did not return here to balance out something you did before but rather because you wanted to evolve yourself through mass and to complete yourself in the emotions gained from experiencing this plane.

You are here to learn that wherever you are, you are there for no other reason than you want to be there. It is your will to be there. You are here to reconcile wisdom and to implement it upon the platform of life. You are here in this lifetime — and however many more lifetimes you wish to be here — to play out this illusion and to experience all the things that your soul needs in order to fulfill itself in wisdom. And when you have gained the rich vapor of emotion from your experiences upon this plane, you will no longer need or desire to return here. And only you determine when you are finished here; no one else does.

You are here, master, to become God. And to become that, you must remove from your being every law, every dogmatic belief, every ritualistic practice and become unlimited in your thought processes. If you desire unlimited freedom of expression — a body that will never die and the peace and joy of being — know that the life you are living is completely unlimited. When you know that, so it will become, for whatever you desire and whatever you know as a truth in your being, so it will be. That is the only law you need ever accept within your kingdom.

Know that you will never have to pay for anything that you have ever thought or done in this or any life as long as you forgive yourself for it. Forgiveness of self is the divine act that removes from your soul the guilt and judgment of self that limit the expression of the God that you are. Once you have forgiven yourself, know that this life and those to come are simply for the experience of being a part of the Now that is the future of all that is.

Know that you are forever, that you have never failed, and that the only thing you have ever done wrong is believing that you have done something wrong.

Love yourself, master, and listen to what self says, what it needs to feel, and then pursue it heartily until you are bored with it. Boredom is a sign from your soul that you have learned all there is to learn from an experience and that it is time to go on to another adventure. When you listen only to the feelings within you, then you are free to become in this moment whatever you choose to become. And know that you never have to answer to any law, any teaching, or any entity. Now — and the feelings that you gain from it — is all that will ever be important.

Become lawless, master. That does not equate recklessness. It means that the ropesman will take the rope away from your throat and allow you to breathe. When you remove yourself from laws and dogma and limited beliefs, then you are allowing yourself to be the freedom and unlimitedness that God is. Then you can simply be the power that you are, to create and regenerate yourself and life. Then the reason that you are here is not to make amends to whomever you did whatever to, but rather because you want to live. And that adventure unfolds moment to moment to moment.

Live and be happy. That is the only thing the Father has ever asked you to do.

***

CHAPTER 14

Purpose In Life

God's only desire for you is that you know and become joy,
for that is the only way you will come to know the Father
and to be as he is.

In each of your lives upon this plane, what is your purpose in being here? Many are reared to think they must be a certain entity or a certain profession, and they are scrupulously watched by family and society to make sure they become it. How ominous. Then there are those who imagine they have been sent here to be a great teacher or savior or healer of mankind. How noble. And there are many others indeed who feel they are here to plod along a carefully laid-out, narrow and holy path to God. How boring.

No one has a purpose when he comes to this plane. The Father has not given you or anyone else a directive as to what your life should be, save for one thing — and that one desire for you provides the ultimate in being — and that is for you to be joyful, whatever joy means to you. For the happier and more joyful you are within your precious and divine self, the closer you are to being the likeness of God and in harmony with all life.

To be happy and joyous is the Father's only desire for you. It is indeed the grandest emotional value there is. It is the greatest accomplishment in life. To have understood and become joy is the only destiny that God has given to all mankind — whatever plane they are upon, whatever understanding they have achieved — for when you have returned to a state of joy and happiness, you have returned to a state of God, for joy is what the Father is. It is an Isness that is in joy at all times.

The Father has given you the power to create whatever you desire, from the vilest of things to the greatest beauty of things. He will become anything you desire him to be in your search for understanding joy. And will he ever judge your actions or the fulfillment of your desires? Nay, he never will. That is the love of Father to son, life force to life force. All he wants you to do is whatever it takes to be happy, joyful, for that is the only way you will come to know the Father and to be as he is.

What is joy? Joy is the freedom of movement without interruption. It is the freedom of expression without judgment. It is the freedom of being without fear or guilt. Joy is knowing that you are creating life on your own terms. It is the sublime movement of self allowed. That is joy.

Why is joy the grandest state of being? Because when you are in a state of joy, you are in the flow of what God is and, in that flow, there is no room for jealousy, anger, bitterness, or war. It is difficult to hate anyone — it is difficult to besiege anyone; it is difficult to hurt anyone — when you are in a state of joy. When you are happy and joyful, you love God seen in all things.

In an exuberant state of joy, you are at peace with everything about you. When you are in joy with life, you cannot feel remorseful or insecure, fearful, angry, or lacking. In a state of joy, you are fulfilled and complete, and life, wisdom, and creativity flow like a mighty river from within your being. In a state of joy, you are inspired to the heights of greatness and the depths of feeling.

In a state of joy, life becomes the fervor and intensity of a dawn when the sky is the most beauteous color of rose, the clouds are tinged with fiery red, and birds are singing in the trees. In joy, you cease to age and will live forever, for life is no longer a drudgery but a wondrous adventure that you only hunger for more of. When joy is apparent, you are at one within your kingdom of self. In a state such as that, you have found utopia.

How do you become joyful? By knowing that every moment of your life gives you the freedom and opportunity to express joy, if that is your desire, and by knowing there is nothing that is ever worth separating yourself from happiness and joy and God — nothing — and by loving yourself completely through and through, for you love God when you do.

There is no greater love in life than the love of self. There is no greater love, for it is from that embrace of self that freedom exists. And it is from that freedom that joy is born. And it is from that birth that God is seen, known, and embraced. The greatest, deepest, most meaningful love is the love of the pure and innocent self, the magnificent creature that sits within the walls of flesh, that moves and contemplates, creates, allows, and is. And when you love who you are — however you are — then you will know this magnificent essence that I love, that is behind all of the faces and within all things. Then you will love as God loves. Then it is easy to love. Then it is easy to forgive. Then it is easy to see God in all life.

When you love who you are, there is no thing unconquerable, no thing unreachable. When you truly love yourself, you live only in the light of your own laughter and travel only the path of joy. When you are in love with yourself, then that light — that united force, that happiness, that jolliness, that mirthful state of being — extends itself to all humanity. And when love abounds within your wondrous being, the world with all of its displeasures becomes beautiful — life becomes meaningful and takes on joy — and joy, through the exuberance of your being, uplifts and glorifies all life and declares your being pure.

There is no greater purpose in life than to live for the love and fulfillment of self, and that can only be achieved by participating in this life and doing those things which bring you happiness, regardless of what they are, for who shall say it is wrong or that it is not good for you. God would never say that, for he will be every direction you turn and the result of everything you experience. And don't ask others what they think. What would they know of joy when their lives have been burdened by the same limitations that have plagued yours.

The Father presses joy to you. He is always there, waiting

for you to open up to receive it. That is what is meant by "Ask and you shall receive." It is quite simple to have joy at all times. Know you are worth it.

Joy begets joy, for when you accept the joy that is pressed to you, that joy heightens the joy of your tomorrows and opens you up for ever greater receivership. That is why loving yourself every moment is imperative, for when you do that, that sets the pace, if you will, for the moments to come. When you live only for the love and joy of self — by always asking yourself what makes you happy and then doing what your feelings tell you, whatever it is — those moments of ecstasy and exhilaration are recorded in the soul of your being, which will create even more moments of happiness and joy in the moments to come.

The more moments you spend being happy and joyful and loving yourself and allowing yourself to be, the closer you are to being the God force of all life. If you will live your life in such a manner — that everything you pursue in life, you pursue to make yourself happy — you will live your life to its grandest destiny. You will achieve miraculous things. You will be a remarkable example of the love of self and God. You will experience and understand the grand beauty and the wonderful enigma that you are. And, behold, in what is termed the final analysis, you will have seen the face of God by realizing that it is your own. Then you are off to another eternity of life experience in a new and grander understanding.

You know, in my time we were called soulless by the Atlatians. Do you know what our search was for then? It was not for a purpose; it was to find a soul that we were told we did not have. I was a wretched barbarian and I hated man. But when I found out what joy was and that I was worth having it, I became the essence that supports and nourishes and is all life.

The only path to the Father is whatever you declare as your joy. That is the only way you get there. That is what takes you back home to God.

Student: Is it true that I chose to come back into a body?
Ramtha: Who else would choose for you?
Student: Then can you tell me why I chose this time and

this place to come back to?

Ramtha: To experience life in this time and this place.

Student: But was there some special purpose that I came here to accomplish and that's why I chose to come back here?

Ramtha: The special purpose, master, is the privilege of experiencing life.

Student: So it can be anything?

Ramtha: It can be anything. But it is no specific thing. You came back here simply to experience life. You chose you, and why not you? You chose this time, and why not? This is a wonderful time. Life is in bloom now. You are in bloom now.

You know, living has become such an overlooked and unappreciated experience, that everyone looks for something other than life to do. But your first and foremost reason for being here is simply to live. The most glorious thing you can achieve in this life, master, is living through it. Is that not a truth? What would a grandiose king be if he did not first have life to become one? Being a king was not his purpose. He only did that because he decided it would be a jolly good thing to do. The most important thing was that he lived to the point that he could become one.

Your greatest accomplishment in life will be living through it. That is perhaps not precisely the understanding that you are wanting to hear but I assure you, master, when you come close to dying, you will appreciate that answer.

Everyone thinks that they must have an excuse for their existence. "Ah, master," they say unto me, "what is my destiny here, my purpose in this life? I know there is a reason I am supposed to be here." So I tell them, "Life," and they are most perplexed and unhappy, for they are waiting to hear of a very elaborate plan where they will rise above a great mount and be draped in gold, with birds singing around their head, and they shall be the salvation of humanity.

Your purpose, master, is simply to live. Whatever you do thereafter will be an extension of your beauty and a contribution to the overall expansion of life. When you realize that living is the most important thing, that that is how you gain your points, as it were, and that you are here because you desire to be here — you want to be here, that you of your own being found it a pleasurable place to return to — then everything else will be understood.

Everyone comes into this existence because they want to live and express here. That is the priority of all humanity. That is the priority of the Father that lives within you. What occurs thereafter is not the obligation to be any specific thing but to be as much as you can in each moment of life. It is called creation, and that you are bound to do because the God within you presses you to create.

You are not here for any destiny but to live and, in every moment of living, to do what the creative self — the soul — urges you to do. From that, anything is possible within the realms of creation. You can create kingdoms untold, lives untold. You can fulfill yourself. You can become whatever you desire to become when you have allowed yourself that explicit freedom. And once you find out that you are worth experiencing it all, you can put forth your light into any fulfillment that pleases you, at any moment that pleases you.

Do you know why some of the most enlightened entities upon your plane are bums living in "bumdom"? Because they live in the moment and do only what they need to do in order to live and go on to the next place. So they have been many places, seen and done many things, and met many entities. Thus they have harvested great knowledge and understanding of the human spirit from many directions. They are very enlightened in their state — and very happy in their state — for they have given themselves the freedom to come and go as they choose. You say to me, "But, master, they have no purpose." Their purpose is to live in the moment and frolic in doing something new and adventurous whenever they feel like it.

This life, master, was not created to be a prison. It was designed to be a platform for creativity and expression that is colorful and challenging and upon which you may have many interludes and adventures, but always because they bring you joy.

Student: But, Ramtha, ever since I was small, I have had this feeling that I want to leave here, that this isn't my home, that there is someplace else.

Ramtha: But there is someplace else. Life is continuous on many different levels and in many places. That is a truth. But I will tell you another truth: If you truly did not want to be here, you would not have come back. The life force within your being is here to experience this life in order to learn and gain happiness from it. Do you think that you are a higher entity who came here only to find this a miserable place to be? A higher entity finds happiness wherever he is.

When times upon this plane become difficult, it is good perhaps to think of going to other places, for that makes life here a bit more bearable. But eventually we realize that we make wherever we are however we choose to make it: good or bad, happy or unhappy, exciting or mundane. It is only our attitudes and our judgments that determine our experiences in life.

This is a wondrous place to be a part of. The Father flourishes here, as he flourishes in all places, as he is all places. When you learn that, master, you will be a wise woman. A greater virtue than knowing that there is another place is taking this life and making it the grandest you can, experiencing every part of this life and loving it. Then you are filled with this life. Then when you leave this plane, there will be nothing here that you need to come back to experience.

Those who come here with one little direction and stay with that direction, because it is socially acceptable here, suffer at the time of death from agony and regret that they should have done this, they should have done that, they should have loved this one and married that one. All of those should-haves will bring them back here to experience all of the now-can-haves until they are filled with all of that. Then they return no more.

Student: But then I came back because I had a should-have, and I don't know what that is.

Ramtha: Master, it is living. If that is too simple to understand, then create for yourself a reason for living and pursue it heartily. But when you have fulfilled it, what will you live for then? Another reason, and on and on and on.

Student: So there's no particular thing that I came back

for, that I might miss accomplishing this time?

Ramtha: My beautiful master, wisdom is accumulated emotion. That is what makes each entity different from all others who come to this plane. You will not experience the things you have already experienced and understood, for you will have no desire to. The things that you have yet to understand — adventures that hold the promise of fulfillment and wisdom — you will always be drawn to, for they will excite you, tempt you, intrigue you, puzzle you. If you will simply allow yourself to be and listen to the urgings within your being, the feelings within you, you will always be experiencing what you are most needing in order to expand your wondrous self into greater wisdom and perpetual joy.

Now, master, let me give you this understanding to perhaps help you with your perplexity. If you are needing a reason for being, let the reason be the one thing that will be with you throughout eternity, and that is called love of self. Love for yourself will survive into eternity, while the purpose of being a this or a that will be fulfilled in this life, only to be replaced by something else. What is the only thing that will be with you for always? Whatever you can add to yourself that will expand you into greater wisdom and more profound love for yourself, and that is doing whatever will make you the greatest that you can be in your own eyes, the most discriminating eyes there are. That will last forever. You, master, are the purpose in life.

When everyone goes beyond thinking that they must do this or that — or that their destiny is this or that, and they get down to the business of being, living explicitly in the moment — they will find a grander happiness and a greater freedom than they have ever known before, a release into life and how it should truly be lived.

That is your purpose — to be.

***

CHAPTER 15

Forgotten Divinity

*When man is told often enough that he is not divine, it
becomes a steadfast belief, for man, the timid seeker of truth,
wishing so desperately to be accepted, will listen to any folly.*

Once man knew of his heritage and his lineage. Once
man knew God not as an essence apart from his being but as the
sublime Isness of ongoing life and thought that was the very life
force of his divine and eternal self. Once man knew that. He
erected great pyramids to stand throughout the ages as reminders
to humanity of the fire within, the God within man. Despite all
the things that have happened throughout your history, those
pyramids still stand as symbols of the greatness and divineness
of man.

In man's beginnings on this plane — when man still knew
he was God — he lived in the same embodiment for thousands
of years because the power that gave the body immortality was
the purity of unlimited thought that man expressed in a state of
being.

Man, God/man, began to forget that he was God even in
his first life experience on this plane. Why? Because he loved
this wonderful playground of matter, and experiencing and
creating here became all that was important. And in his endeavor
to express his creativity here — and to maintain the vehicle that
allowed him to do that — man, the magnificent creature of
unlimited thought processes, began to experience the limited
thoughts of survival, jealousy, and possessiveness.

Man's being — his soul and Spirit —is forever. Nothing
can ever change that. But the embodiment that the Gods created

for themselves from the clay of the earth is vulnerable to the thoughts of the immortal being who occupies it. Whatever thought man accepts and allows himself to feel will manifest in the body, for the embodiment is the last part of man's kingdom and is supported by the thought processes of the God who inhabits it.

When God/man began to experience attitudes of survival, he began to lessen his power of thought to spark an eternal life force within the body. Thus the body began to fail. As the body began to fail, it lessened man's ability to reason through his brain. As man began to lose his power to reason, fear began to engross his consciousness. As the element of fear became an attitude within man's thought processes, the embodiment began to suffer from the force and effects of fear: disease, illness, death.

Although the first civilizations on your plane were endowed with great enlightenment, the unlimitedness of their thought processes began to dim into limitedness through the expectancy of death and the attitudes of survival. Those attitudes of survival, arising from the fear of death, would be passed on to future generations as what is termed instincts for survival, for whatever man thinks becomes patterned within his cellular and genetic structures.

The Gods entered into the limitations of matter out of the desire to experience their creativity through the bodily form. But when the Gods, as man, experienced attitudes of limitation upon this plane, they unknowingly became locked into the bodily experience, for when each God experienced the death of his first embodiment, he entered into what is called a Void. This Void was a place — a dimension of light — that was neither back into a consciousness understanding of all-knowing God, nor was it back upon the plane of matter. The God could no longer return to the plane of unlimited thought, for now he maintained within his thought processes the alteredness of attitudes of limitation.

In order for the God to continue to advance in life — and finding this playground of matter to be a wonderful experience — he was most anxious to return here. So the God came back into another embodiment through the seed of his own offspring, in order to continue to express in matter and to reconcile all of the limited thoughts he had permitted to alter his thought processes in the previous life. But as he began to experience more of the material aspects of this plane, the God experienced further alteredness and fell deeper and deeper into limitation. Thus began the cycle of reincarnation upon the plane of demonstration.

As the Gods returned here as man again and again — in order to continue their adventures in life — this plane gradually became their whole concept of life and they forgot their lineage and their divinity. No longer did they conceive God to be allness, all thoughts. No longer did they maintain the knowingness that they could return, if they desired, to the plane of pure thought, unlimited being, the plane of consciousness that they had expressed upon from their beginning. They reasoned that they could experience only limited spheres, limited thoughts. Thus other planes of expressed consciousness emerged as what is termed limited heavens, limited spheres. There, upon the death of the embodiment, entities who had forgotten the grandest and simplest of all planes could experience life according to their happiness and collective-attitude thinking.

When the Gods, as man, no longer knew that they were divine and immortal and that all-power and all-knowingness truly were within them, they began to be vulnerable to the egos of those around them. Soon there rose up entities who sought to elevate themselves above others by saying that only they, through their mystical powers and immeasurable source of knowledge, had the understanding of God. Since man had become a fearful and herdlike creature, these seers and prophets and oracles sought to enhance their power by issuing forth prophecies of doom and peril. And if the people did not pay particular attention to what the seers had to say, they issued forth curses and threats of damnation.

Thus was religion born upon this plane to further separate man from his internal beauty, his eternal godship. And religion was very clever, for it did not have to govern and rule peoples through the sword. It had only to perpetuate the teaching that God was not within their reach; that all-knowingness and all-power were not within them.

Now the soul is forever memory. It remembers all experiences of all lives. Whatever man is told often enough — no matter how altered an understanding it is — will eventually become a steadfast reality, for man, the timid seeker of truth, wishing so desperately to be accepted, will listen to any folly. So if you tell man long enough that God is outside of him and that he is wretched and evil in his soul, these thoughts become steadfast understandings within man's soul memory, and they will be very difficult to change. And that is indeed what occurred over thousands of years on this plane. These simple entities, coming from one life back into another, continually fell under the auspices of these teachings. And they became so conditioned to the understanding that they were wicked — and that God was outside of their beings — that they came to know absolutely that they were other than divine, and that the only way to know God, to go back to God, was through the rule of prophets and priests and religious organizations.

When man no longer accepted his own knowingness to be the essence of truth, he gave away his sovereignty and power and became a part of a collective mass, which permitted religions and governments through the ages to rule people as if they were one entity. But they are not. All are unique Gods with unique destinies to fulfill and adventures to experience. Man is entitled to his adventures.

When man accepted the teaching that he is wretched and a sinner and that the Father is outside of him, he completely separated himself from God. And it is that understanding and belief acceptance that has brought man back into an embodiment over and over again, for as long as man has the thinking that he is other than divine, that the Father is not within him, then he is doomed in a sense to be born a million times until he realizes his divinity and lives once again in a state of being.

Incarnation was never meant to be an entrapment. It was never meant to be everlasting. It was simply a game to participate in, a new adventure in the exploration of creativity and life. But you quickly lost yourself in the senses of the embodiment and your body became your whole identity. You became so immersed in the matter of this plane that you became man, the insecure, man, the fearsome, man, the vulnerable, man, the dying element, because you forgot the powerful essence within you. Thus you learned of death, but you forgot life. You learned of sorrow, but you forgot joy. You learned of man, but you forgot God, your sublime intelligence, that allows you to create your illusions however you choose.

All of you have lived many lives upon this plane: some of you, thirty thousand lives; some of you, ten thousand; some of you, only two. That is how many times you have lived and died. And though your lives upon this plane have been only a dream, a game, an illusion in the adventure of life, they have corrupted you greatly. You have lived so many lives in which you have been reminded — by family, by society, by religion, and by governmental powers — that you are wretched and that God is not within your reach, that it has become the steadfast reality of your thought processes.

To this day most of you still do not know that God is you, that you possess within you the power to know and be all things. Thus you let teachers and religions and everyone else rule your life and interpret truth for you. You allow the understanding of others to complicate and clutter the simple truth that has been spoken for ages in your time, that the Father and the kingdom of heaven are indeed within you. What grander truth can be written than that? But many of you who do not know that still think you must go through dogma and certain mechanics, as it were — rituals, prayers, chants, fasts, meditations — in order to connect with God and become enlightened. Yet the more you do these things, the more you convince your soul that you are not what you are trying to become, that you are far from the love of God and the understanding you are seeking, for you are having to do arduous things in order to achieve it.

Now religion is not wrong. Those who have set up and furthered religious teachings are your beloved brothers who, in seeking to understand their own divinity, their own worth and power, have enslaved their brothers, thus enslaving themselves. What they have done, as harmful as it has been, has been their truth for their experience and understanding. I am a lover of all people, even the priests and seers, for they are God also.

Practicing rituals and following dogma are not wrong, but it will never feel completely right because the voice within you — that is God — says that you already are what you are struggling to reach.

I have returned here simply to tell you that there is a better way and also to tell you that you are already God, and that you have never failed, and you have never done anything wrong, and you are not miserable, wretched creatures, and you are not sinners, and there is no wonderful folly called a devil. When you realize these things, then you can get down to the business of being happy, which is what God is. The Father is not an angry, mournful, meditative, pious creature. It is the essence that is complete and infinite joy.

I tell you, God is within you. It has been there in all of your lives. You are already God, for that is the divine, creative intelligence that sits within the cavity of your being, the essence that has loved you into experiencing limitation and will love you back into unlimitedness once again.

Limitation has been an adventure. It has been an experience, and most on this plane are experiencing it greatly. Unfortunately, you forgot that there is something better, and you made limitation a way of life. If you only knew that through unlimited thinking you could transcend the embodiment and all universes and planes, you would never choose to be limited again. If you only knew that and allowed yourself to receive and embrace all thoughts, you would have joy and peace in life beyond your grandest dreams.

Thought is the ultimate creator. Whatever you think and then allow yourself to feel becomes the reality of your life. Every thought you embrace that goes beyond the spectrum of limited thinking, so shall it manifest for a broadening or widening of your life. All it takes is opening up your thought processes to accept ever more unlimited thoughts in order for you to go beyond limited man into unlimited God.

Just as you have become the knowingness that you are

wretched within your being, if you now know that you are God within your being, so will you become God in your totality. In order to go back to what is now termed a seventh-level understanding of pure thought, to the ultimate state of being — a state in which you are the ultimate power of all things — the only thing you need is simply to know that the Father lives within you, for the memory that you are God sits within the soul of your being. It is there, dormant in your soul, waiting to be recognized, ready to become an experienced reality. It becomes that by knowing. When you know you are God, that feeling of certainty will create the experiences and the understanding that will teach you that your knowingness is a truth. No one can give you that knowingness. Only you can achieve that understanding through your own thought processes and emotional being.

When you know that God and you are one, you remove from your thought processes the attitudes of separateness and you unite with your godhead once again. When you realize that the all-wise, all-knowing intelligence of the Father is the totality of thought — the basis of all things that are — and allow yourself to be all thoughts, then you are all that God is, which is all things. Then you return to your freedom, your greatness, and your glory. Then you do not have to return to this heaven over and over again but can go on to greater heavens and grander adventures that await you.

I tell you, there is nothing you must accomplish on this plane except being who and what you are, for the knowingness that you are God is achieved in a state of being, for God is beingness. It is the Isness of all life. To be in a state of being — a state of allowing yourself simply to be who you are, however you are expressing — is to be completely as the Father is, and that you can accomplish in a moment. In a moment it is realized.

God is this Now. Infinity is this Now. To be forever God is to live wholly in the eternity of this Now, for that is how God lives. Simply be. Then you are one with the Isness and ongoingness of all life, and your body will elevate itself to become that ongoingness. Then you do not have to die but can transcend all planes to the seventh, which is the conclusiveness of all things, thought. That is a truth.

Man is beginning to come out of limitation because there are many upon your plane who are questioning their lives and why they are slaves to the hypocrisy of government, of dogma, of society, and where in turn they lead. They are beginning to love themselves and others enough to see beyond the film of limited consciousness and to rise above it. They are awakening to the understanding that there is an essence that lies within them and within all people that is gentle and loving and wise. They are beginning to realize that all of the prophesies — and all of the tales and all of the fears — that have governed mankind for so long have not manifested; they have outlived them all. They are questioning who they are and why, if they are to love God, must they be frightened of him.

Consciousness on this plane is changing. The limitations of understanding which have caused man to be a beastly creature, generation after generation after generation, are being lifted to permit man to be the sublime God essence that he is.

It is time to have a new learning occur, which is really not new at all. Deep within your soul, you will know what the truth is because the truth will permit you to see beyond the stagnation of dogmatic beliefs into the heaven of thought and understanding that has been there all along. As the rope is removed from around your throat, and the feelings of joy begin to surface and become eminent within your soul, you will begin to be this magnificent God that you are, in a state of being.

This age of yours is ending. This has been the Age of Flesh. The new age is already on the horizon, and it is called the Age of Light, the Age of Pure Spirit, the Age of God. It is the age when man knows that all are equal and that the kingdom of heaven has always been within him. The Age of Light shall take man back into unlimited thought, back into a sublime kingdom of love and joy and freedom in being. Those who will be the new kingdom will not be the warlords and tyrants amongst men but the heralds of peace who are rising above the stagnation of limitation to say, "I am God, and all whom I see do I love, for I am all I see and I love what I am." Each who comes to that understanding will lift the whole of consciousness by his one solitary light. And one by one you will return to a state of unlimitedness, rich with the pearls of wisdom, that will allow you to create more wisely in the eternity to come.

Your lives upon this plane have been a grand illusion. They have been a great dream. But you will emerge from the dream learned, understanding God. Everyone will. One day you will glance up to a sky that has become very cloudy. As you look into your heavens, you will see a blaze of brilliant lights flickering all around, and you will think the stars themselves have come to nestle within the clouds. What you will see is what all mankind is going to see. It will help you to awaken from your slumber and realize that all I am teaching you is indeed a grand truth and a wonderful reality.

Student: I would like to know how we became separated from God and the things that unified us in our beginning. How did that happen?

Ramtha: In your very beginning, when each of you knew that you were one with the Father, your ego — your identity — was God in a singular uniqueness and life was the emotional adventure into the experience of all thoughts, for God is all thoughts. Your ego was pure and unaltered, for no attitudes were maintained within your being which would limit the acceptance of thought or God into your being. You knew that you were forever in the Now moment of being and were unlimited in your ability to receive thought from the Father, transmute it into emotion, and manifest the emotion into creativity.

All of you were like little children, for you did not possess any attitude that would alter the purity of your beings or limit your expression. You did not know fear. You did not know judgments of greater or lesser. You did not know competitiveness or jealousy or possessiveness. You did not know death. You were like little children, for you had not experienced any of these attitudes.

Now you, the Gods, from your very beginning possessed the powerful drive to create, to express the emotion of thought into creative forms. And the power to do that was not given a little more to one and a little less to another. All were equal. But as soon as you began to create, a competitive spirit arose within you, the drive to take the thought of another's creativity and expand it into something greater, to create more, thought by thought by thought. Why do you think there are so many species of flowers on your plane? You would think that one rose would have been enough. And how many more butterflies could there possibly be?

Why did the Gods become a competitive race? Because in their drive to create, they began to contemplate that perhaps their creativity was not as grand as another's. Thus they began to see themselves as lessened within their beings. And to compensate for that feeling of lessness, the Gods sought to outdo each other's creations. And the more they embroiled their thought processes in competitive creativity, the more they saw themselves as less than the perfection of Isness, as separate from God, which is the equality of all things.

You see, separateness from life and the understanding called imperfection come about only when something is seen as greater than something else. Yet in the reality of life, no thing is greater or less than anything else. All things simply are, in an equality of Isness. Thus everything is in a state of perfection or, more appropriately, a state of Isness, of being. It is only attitudes, collective thoughts, that make something less than the perfection of Isness that it truly is.

Now your greatest separation occurred when you entered into the embodiment of man. Up to that point, even though you had begun to separate yourself from all things, you were still aware of your godhood and immortality of being. But when you lowered yourself into an embodiment and began to experience the realities of cellular matter, you entrapped yourself in the functions of mass called hunger, cold, and survival, the struggle to maintain that which you had become. You had now become intertwined with cellular matter, which was programmed in its creation to permit the survival of the mass. That marriage of a great immortal being with a mechanism of mass, oriented to the survival of its own structure, greatly altered your ego state of being. That is when the tree of knowledge, the altered ego, was born. And it was the experience of the emotions of fear, competitiveness, and jealousy on this plane — recorded in your soul and programmed into your body's cellular structures — that further intensified your altered ego, that further altered the knowingness that you were divine, immortal, and one with all life.

Student: I still don't understand why the Gods, who had always known that they were forever, ended up believing that they would die. How did they come to accept the idea of death in the first place?

Ramtha: They accepted and understood the processes of change — what you term death — from the very things they had created. You see, many things created here were designed to feed upon one another, for the substance that each creation needed to sustain itself had to be of the same substance as itself. It is what you term a food chain.

So the flora became foodstuffs for the animals that the Gods had created. And when the animals partook of the plants, the Gods who created the plants saw to their horror that their creations had been resolved before their eyes and transmuted into yet another energy. The animals would then be food for yet other animals that were created by another God to be greater than the first, and on and on. It was one way that the Gods chose to compete with one another. You see, it was most humiliating to have your creation eaten up and digested by another God's creation.

Death was further understood, master, through the process of designing and evolving the embodiment of man. In order to perfect the creature called man, the Gods became a part of it, as they had become a part of all things they had created here. Since their earliest versions of man were not very agile creatures, the animals were continuously partaking of the body of man and finding him quite a delicacy at that. So through that, the Gods experienced and understood the action called death. That understanding enabled them to improve upon the embodiment to make it more forceful against death at the hands of their very own creations, the animals of carnivorous nature.

Now man's romance with a God outside of his being began when the Gods had a romance with this plane, with their desire to experience and interact with all of the things they had created here. The Gods had been the plants. They had been the animals. They had been the insects. They had been everything. But to have a form that had dominion over all things, that was their ultimate love and creation.

When the Gods ultimately formed themselves into man and woman — and all of their attentions were focused on outsmarting and escaping from their creations — they became into an altered state of life. The irony was even if they escaped from the animals that preyed upon them, they could not escape the attitudes of survival that were beginning to engross their consciousness. It was their attitudes of survival and the fear of death that eventually brought their bodies down, for whatever one fears, he will become.

You know, of all the things the Gods ever created, nothing is more devastating than the creation called fear, for no thing can express life in its shadow.

Now when the Gods, as man, experienced death, their only reality and their only desire were to continue to experience this paradise of matter and to create more in this kingdom as an accomplishment, for the Gods' egos were great. Thus the Gods eagerly came back to become better and better and better, to reconcile the lessness they had perceived in themselves, and to express moreness in their creativity here. Through the attitude and the desire to become better, they became so immersed in the matter of this plane that they forgot they were divine and immortal and became death and dying objects. Yet the understanding of being one with all life had begun to be lost, unfortunately, in the designing of creation — even before the Gods had a love affair with this plane — through competition and the thoughts of greaterness or moreness.

I tell you this, master: Your oneness is truly only a moment — a breath — away. When you within the depths of your being no longer wish to be separate from any one thing, you no longer will be. It is simply your attitude, your limited thinking, your altered identity that has separated you from all thought. When you come back into all thought by removing judgment against thought, then you will never again be lost or separated. Then you will be a light to many others who will find their way back into an alignment with the Father.

Student: Ramtha, I can understand that we are all actually perfect, that we are God, and that we do live forever. But that doesn't seem to lessen the feeling I have at times that I need to be careful and protect myself. How can I overcome this illusion I have about myself, this feeling that I need to be cautious, which seems to inhibit me from freely expressing who I really am?

Ramtha: You know, master, the animals are endowed with wondrous devices for self-preservation, the primeval instincts for survival that have been programmed into their cellular structures so that they can live, experience, and evolve. Mankind is also endowed with primeval instincts, which have been passed on genetically from seed to seed. Man's instincts for survival are immersed within the body's cellular structures so that he may protect himself, for mankind is born naked. He has not fangs, nor horns, nor swiftness of foot, nor nimbleness of limb, nor is he endowed with acute hearing or grand eyesight. He is a very refined, remarkable, self-contained entity, whose greatest instincts for self-preservation are caution and the seclusion of self. Mankind is endowed with these instincts for, if he were not, he would not have survived to be the wondrous, thinking, evolving, creative mass that he truly is.

When you, as everyone else here, selected to forfeit your freedom of Spirit in order to experience the density of matter, you became intertwined with its genetic, instinctual patterns, one of the conditions of expressing through the matter of this plane. So to be man is to be fearful, herdlike, doubtful, and very cautious. 'Tis a great truth.

Caution is not an illusion; it is a condition of living here as man. That need never be forgiven within self but accepted as a necessary instinct for the preservation of your embodiment.

But take this understanding one step further. Now that you realize your body has protected you in order to allow the tiny, wondrous, creative spark that you are to evolve itself here, it is time for you to go beyond the flesh into the immortal aspects of your Spirit and soul. It is now the moment, if you will, for the Spirit of your being to take hold of your body and protect it through an unlimitedness of thought understanding.

What is to be done now is to become you, God that you are: steadfast, certain, sovereign, I Am. And the only illusion you need to master is the illusion that you do not have the ability to become that. And how do you remove that illusion? Simply by removing it from your thought processes. Whatever you do in thought and in feeling is reality, even if it is never manifested into the reality of this dimension. Once you have embraced the thought that you are God, the I-Am principle, you have already become it.

Love what you are, master. Love it. Know that you are forever, that you are God. Know it. Feel it. Embrace that thought. When the instinctual heritage that has protected you through the ages confronts the knowingness that you are indeed immortal rather than mortal, that you are indeed unlimited God rather than limited man, your soul will pass this unlimited thought on to the cellular mass of your embodiment, and the cellular mass will be in jubilation. Then your body will conform happily to the unlimited thoughts of the great God that occupies it. And inasmuch as your body has had uncertainty and caution for its instinctual existence, it shall now have God unlimited within its cells, such that the matter of the body can be unified into an alignment with the totality of God I Am.

To be more you, master, is simply to reach beyond the boundaries of your uncertainty. And when you, who have been protected by your embodiment, claim dominion over all that is within your understanding, the body will happily follow.

Love yourself, master, completely. Love life, all of it. When you do, you will come back into your union, I assure you, simply through an attitude and in but a moment. That is all it takes. Simply know.

***

CHAPTER 16

Reincarnation

You came back to experience God, to understand self, to
live the principles of I Am. And the principles of I Am
encompass every emotion created in the realms of thought.

Student: I didn't come with any specific questions for
you. I felt that whatever you said to anyone would certainly be
applicable to all of us.

Ramtha: It is, and it has been.

Student: But I would like to ask you two general questions.
You said that when we leave this plane, we always go on to
something better.

Ramtha: That is correct. Yet when you leave this
audience, you will go on to a greater moment in being, for your
life advances every moment to be grander than the moment before.

Student: Well, could you tell us something about the
mechanics of reincarnation. I mean, why would we leave here
for something better and yet return here once again? Are we sent
back here to learn something?

Ramtha: First, master, how would you know that there is
not something better awaiting you here in a future time?

Student: Because it seems that it's a struggle to live here,
and there is a lot of pain and sadness to deal with. Even though
we may not be experiencing a great deal of pain ourselves, we
see it all around us. So there's a lot of pain here, obviously, and
it's difficult to imagine it getting much better in the near future.

Ramtha: You know, the last pain here was starvation,

and everyone was always hungry. The thing then was to work arduously in order to make a pence or a rupee or a shekel to buy a loaf of bread, a bit of cheese, and rotted wine to fill an empty belly. Now look at everyone. They are all trying to fight off their fat. Now that everyone has been fed and has gotten plump, along comes someone who says, "Tsk, tsk, tsk. That is not beautiful." So now everyone is struggling to be starved again. Is life not an adventure?

The pain here, master, is called ego.

Student: Okay, but I'm not sure that I follow your point. You seem to be saying that life is circular. Is there no end to the circle?

Ramtha: Life does not go in a circle, master, nor does it ever repeat itself. It always changes, and yet it evolves every moment to be constant. Life is all-encompassing and creates the next moment by virtue of its own being, its own Isness. It is created in the moment by each entity according to his attitude. It is the attitude toward life that allows its cycles of change to seem circular.

Reincarnation is indeed a truth. It is simply laying down one body — because the attitude permitted it to die — and taking up another one, either here or somewhere else upon the plane of matter.

Why does anyone come back here? Because they want to. Do you think that you are made to come back here — that you are kicked from whatever plane you are on back into an embodiment — only to have to struggle through the birth canal and become completely dependent upon the egos around you?

There was no edict that sent you here, master, for there is no one who can ever make you do anything against your will. You are the one who decided to return here. You are the one who desired to express again upon this plane. So if you are looking for someone to blame your miseries on, you will have to look yourself in the eye. You are wholly responsible for your own beauty, your own being, your own sorrowful or wonderful life. And it is about time that that is the way it is known.

No one is ever forced to reincarnate upon this plane. But

after living here for eons, man begins to think that this is all there is. And when he loses his body and is away from his emotional attachments and the toys that are here, he soon wants to hurry up to get back here, for he thinks that this is the only heaven there is. And so for him it is.

The only reason you are here is because you want to be, because you have a need within your being to fulfill here. And the need is to express joy, or sorrow, or pity, or anger, or pain, or anything else you wish to experience on this plane of illusion so that you may have as much of it as you want. Then when you become tired of it or bored with it, you can change your attitude and experience some other emotion. It is as simple as that.

Can utopia live alongside pain and sorrow and hellish situations? Indeed it can. It is only an attitude away.

You came back here to experience God, to understand self, to live the principles of I Am. And the principles of I Am encompass all that everyone is, every attitude, every emotion, every character, every illusionary situation created in the realms of thought called God.

Do you know why you are the identity you are now? Because you have been most of the other roles before and now you are experiencing this one. Why weren't you born a starving child rather than the opulent entity that you are? Because you have been the starving child who wanted to be the opulent entity, and so you are. And why are you not the baker who bakes the bread to feed his family? Because, master, you have been the baker who baked the bread to feed his family. You are now the entity who purchases it from him.

The wonderful thing about this kingdom is that it is ongoing and changeable, and you can be any player you wish to be. And as you advance upon the platform of life, you advance to plateaus which offer you a stage to play out the illusions that will provide the greatest learning within your being. And upon that stage you have the freedom to become king or pauper, lover or loved, slave or freedman, whatever illusion will provide you the understanding your soul is needing for fulfillment.

There are many experiences you have never had, master,

for there are things you have never done and entities you have never been. There are entities in this world who live in sublime peace and whose needs are simple. And whatever they need, whatever they want, they simply manifest. They live in happiness and joy, master, attitudes and adventures in thought that you have yet to choose for your experience.

There are many understandings you have yet to live. And do you know what the grandest of them is? Living simply for the reason of living. To live simply for the reason of living is the greatest achievement in the understanding of life, for that is when you will know peace. That is when you will know joy. That is when, master, you become God in your totality once again.

You have yet to experience that understanding of life, for you have allowed yourself to be intimidated into a supportive role, a laboring role, a competitive role, an idealistic role, a suffering role, a neurotic role. You have accepted that as your lot, and so it is. But you would realize that those are only minute particums of your options in life, if you ever allowed yourself to go and see the other parts of it.

This life, regardless of all the things that have occurred in your history as mankind, is really quite superb. Unfortunately, those who dwell in cities — amidst the stagnation and thickness of social consciousness — think that this is a miserable, wretched place to live. But if you ever find the courage within your being to get away from ideals and intimidation and the limited consciousness of man and go live in the wilderness — at one with the God within you — you will find that life is really quite splendid, that it is an ongoing, unlimited, beautiful thing.

The reason you have come back here, master, is to live. But you have not broken away from the things that bind you to this plane so that you can experience the majesty of God and life. You have not walked on a glacier, or hidden under a rock bridge, or peered out a window in winter to see a redbird sitting there, brilliant against the snow. Nor have you been in deep caverns, or walked in the desert and watched a snake in its quest for food. And you haven't slept in a great pyramid all alone, or gone on explorations where no one has ever been. And there are many of those places. You haven't sailed a great ocean and watched great fish jump, or followed a deer into a dappled wood.

You have not done many things that are electrifying and thrilling and wonderful to your being. And not one of them would ever care about your labor, or your schooling, or your status, or the age of your auto machine.

Those are facets of life that you have yet to experience. But when you do, they will break down your neuroses, your fears, your traps, and your wonderings. And there will be moments that you will feel like exploding with joy, except you would want somebody there to see you explode and yet you would be intimidated if they were. That is your nature, but there is nothing wrong with that. You just have not allowed yourself to experience all of your options here, for you have been hard-pressed to become an illusionary ideal that is utterly alien to the joy and freedom of life.

Now if you do not want to return here, don't. You do not have to, ever. I never came back, for I ascended with the wind and took with me everything that I was. And in that, I became a free entity — a free entity. That is because I transcended all the things I had done in my life here. I forgave myself and embraced this life and got on with this business of being God. And if an ignorant, wretched barbarian could do it, master, it is a certainty that you can.

The way one finishes his life here is he lives it and loves it and becomes a part of the simple things. And he rids himself of ideals that are intimidating, limiting, and restrictive to the freedom of life. And he lives in the freedom of himself, and loves himself, and ceases to compare himself.

When you cease living for the images of society and live instead for your own ideal, your own truth — however that is within your being, and love your eternal being — then you become one with the flora and the fishes and indeed with all life. Then you can say, "I have finished this experience. I have loved all life that is here and, because I have, I am ready for a new adventure. I am ready for a far-off kingdom and a new understanding and a whole different way of being." When you have done those things, master, you will leave this plane in a blaze of glory. That is how I left.

I am a lover of this plane. I tread its valleys often. I blow in the trees and become part of the laughter of children. I know what this life is, for I have not missed out on the values here. But far greater I know the sufferings of those whom I love above all things, my beloved brothers. And I have the answers, but they are of little use unless applied.

The reason you and everyone else are expressing here is because you want to. That is reincarnation.

Student: Thank you. I will have to think about what you've said.

Ramtha: Do. For when you do, perhaps you will choose to be kinder to your being and allow it the freedom to breathe a bit easier.

Student: I was wondering if you would possibly tell us something about what you do when you're not squeezed into this plane.

Ramtha: I am doing the same thing that you are doing: expressing. The only difference is yours is a limitation of expression and mine is not. I have a reach that goes into forever, for I never contemplate the ending of myself, for there is no such thing. And I indeed go with the wind, for that was my ultimate desire.

I am being happy. And I watch you in your life, and her in hers, and him in his. I look upon your illusions here and — while they are all so serious to you and filled with awesome-colored water— I laugh, for all you have to do is see more. And there is more.

I am expressing, master, and I am being happy with what I am. And when I am not the identity you see of me here, I am that which is: the platform from which all things come forth, for the seventh level is the totality of thought, which is the great Void that holds your planets in orbit, your cells together, and encompasses all things to the perimeters of forever. And when you are a seventh-level entity, there is no such thing as levels. There only is. In that, you become all feeling of all things, of all knowingness, of all thought.

Contemplate what it is like to be thought. How far can a thought travel? Can you lay a thought on the surface of the sun, perhaps on the dark side of the moon, or on the great and small stars in your heavens? Can you send a thought to another entity on another plane? You can do it in less than a moment. You have it right within you to be that. You are the entity that does not want that expression. You are wanting this expression, and so it is.

Student: Certainly there has to be a point when we realize why we keep coming back.

Ramtha: There is. It is called happiness. And that point is obtained when there is no entity you would rather be than yourself and no place you would rather be than right where you are. That is the point of realization.

One other thing, master. What is to you sorrow and misery and pain is oftentimes another entity's happiness. Everyone here is happy with their lives. They don't realize that because their ideal of happiness is a clown that runs around like a little Tinkerbell, changing things into colors of blue and lavender and pink.

Everyone here is happy because everyone is doing exactly what they want to do in accordance with their will. If they are wanting to be ill, they are being ill. If they are wanting to be unhappy, they are being unhappy because they want to be, because that makes them happy. You know, if you force some entities to laugh, they will break down and weep on you.

Everyone here is expressively enjoying life. If they weren't, they would die in a moment. And when their time comes, they do die, for they think they must. One day, master, in joy and the peace of being, you will realize simply by watching everyone around you that everyone is infinitely happy, however they are expressing.

Student: May I ask one more question? You said that I've been different people in other lives. I was wondering if you could tell me who I was in my past lives.

Ramtha: Master, if ever we hold audience to bring forth in explicit detail all of your records, as they are termed, we would be here into your next life. Your lives have numbered twenty thousand, three hundred forty-six and a half. So to tell you of your past, you must decide which time, which land, which illusion; then we could bring it forth.

You know, master, I have found that many of those who consider this life to be mundane or unfeeling often revel in the past, for they see that perhaps the past holds for them a vibrancy of life or the esteem they feel they are lacking. And they fantasize about their past in a most romantic, heroic fashion, for when life here is dull and boring, they can always conclude that they were very heroic in battle and left many women behind weeping for them. And when they did return, the whole town turned out in a celebration that lasted for eons. Or they were more beautiful than any woman in the world at that particular time and had every man as a lover in those days.

Now I will tell you this for all to understand. You have all lived many lives, and those lives have been illustrious and romantic, wretched and barbaric, famous and infamous. But all that you were in your past is not as grand as you are now. In this Now, you are the greatest you have ever been, master, for you are the cumulative knowledge and experience of all the lives you have ever lived. The Now, master, is the purpose for all that was.

You have never been better than you are now, no matter the disguise or the illusion or the experience, for that which you possess in wisdom, knowingness, and love, you have grander now than you ever had. If I were to devance you into five lives before this one, you would not even know who you were because you have refined the element called self to a point beyond the recognition of what it once was. Of the lives which you once lived, if they were to look upon you this day, they would call you gallant, a genius, a heretic. They would call you possessed, because your understanding is far greater than what it was in those days.

It is unwise to look to who you were in your past. When you look back to your past for answers, you will never experience this moment of life and the answers that it holds for your future, for you will be too busy with your head backwards to see the Now when it comes. You are curious about who you have been before, master, yet you don't even know who you are now.

It is good to know we have lived before, for that gives us hope for our tomorrows. But the fundamental beauty that lived all of those experiences is still sitting quiet, pondering, waiting to be awakened to the realization that it is a great God that has the power and the option to create its life and fulfill itself however it chooses.

Learn to live in this Now. Nows are virgin. They are permissive moments. You make the virgin moment whatever you declare it to be through your attitude. You can be displeased, pained, sorrowful, miserable, all in the moment. Or in the next moment you can change your attitude and become lovely and free, enticing, happy, and full of joy and exuberance in that moment. And in the next moment to come, which is unaffected by the previous two, you can become somber, brilliant, dedicated, remorseful, whatever you desire.

What is important, master, is to know who you are now and do something about being happy in this life. If you wish in a future life to have the ability to remember this one, make each moment a memorable one that will always remain lively in your soul. If you wish to live into infinity, you must first learn to live each moment fully.

Student: Could you tell me perhaps what you see in my future?

Ramtha: Who will you be in your future? You will always be you. Though the eyes and the color of skin and the mask will change, you will always be you. You will always have the same soul and the same God Spirit of your being. You will be in your next life whatever illusionary character you decide to portray. And if it is upon this plane, you will go through the birth process and create the fruit of the womb according to your own particular design and see that it fulfills whatever game and illusion you have destined for yourself in that existence. Or you can simply be without the illusion and go on to a grander plane of understanding.

Learn to live in the Now, master. Be grand in this life and experience you. Ride the wind. Sail a thought to the moon. Lay a splendid thought on the sun so that it will know who you are. Sit upon a star. Speak to the water. That is all you. It is all God. It is all life.

Student: Thank you. I have one last question. Could you tell me which plane I am progressing to?

Ramtha: To God, master. You are progressing toward your godship. You are refining your godship. You came here as a God, embroiled yourself in the flesh — into hunger and heat and cold and territorial boundaries — and have forgotten about the divinity, the power, the all-consuming, all-wise intelligence that you are. That has caused your link to this plane, which is also progressing to the seventh.

You are progressing to the seventh understanding, which is knowing God in all things. And the height of that knowingness is the giver of that knowingness, which is you, completely.

Student: So be it.

Ramtha: And so it shall be.

***

CHAPTER 17

The Science Of Knowing

You have the ability to know all that is, for everything that is known is in the great consciousness of God, and the mind of God beats like a heart to pump it to you.

There are many upon your blessed plane who are struggling arduously to be enlightened, as it were, a most worthwhile thing to be. Yet there are few who truly understand what that term means. To be enlightened simply means to be in light of, to have knowledge of, to have knowledge available to you so that you can apply it however you choose.

How do you become enlightened? Not by being anointed. The only way you become enlightened is by allowing thought to enter into your thought processes, embracing it into emotion, and experiencing it into wisdom.

Why is knowledge important? It is your grandest treasure for, when all else has been taken from you, what has not been taken from you and never can be is the knowledge that gives you the ability to create again. When you have knowledge, you have freedom; you have options. When you have knowledge, you can build kingdoms unlimited. When you have knowledge, there is nothing to fear, for then there is no thing, no element, no principality, no understanding that can ever threaten or enslave or intimidate you. When fear is given knowledge, it is called enlightenment.

Knowledge allows your mind to reason and contemplate beyond what you already know. It permits you to see further into the knowingness of all things that are and to grow in your capacity to receive even greater knowledge. Knowledge urges you to expand yourself, to seek an ever-broadening identity, to become. In that, it takes you from the boundaries of a limited life into a more unlimited expanse. Through knowledge and the adventure into learning, you become heightened in simplicity, and in that simplicity will you find peace in being and the joy of life.

Now I wish to give you an understanding of the science of knowing, how you have the ability to know all things. Why is that important? Because whatever you know, you will become. And when you learn how to know all things that are, you become all that is — which is God — completely: unlimited knowingness, unlimited life, the totality of thought. And in that you are, once again, the unlimited freedom and joy of being.

To understand how you can know all that is, you must first understand that not only does everything exist from thought, which is the mind of God, but everything emanates the thought of its being back to the mind of God.

Everything has a light field surrounding it. There is nothing that exists that is not surrounded by a corona of light, for that holds the image of thought and creates the ideal into the form called matter. Through that light field each thing emanates the thought of its being back into what is termed consciousness flow, or the river of thought, which is the mind of God.

Look at the carpet, the plant, the light, the leather in your shoes. Look at your hand or another entity. What do these things have in common? They are all existing. And by virtue of their existing, each emanates from its being not only the thought of its being but also its awareness of everything else around it. It is called collective perception. As the carpet is aware of the colors that are in it or who is sitting upon it, or as the plant is aware of the room, that awareness is emitted through the light of its being into the flow of consciousness. And each moment that awareness will change, for God — the river of thought in which everything exists — is ever-expanding and ever-moving.

Every star system, every particum of dust, every entity seen and unseen from this and all other universes, emanates the thought of its being into the mind of God, for that is where it came from. Everything emanates back to thought. That is how everything is known.

How do you have the ability to know all there is to know? Your physical body is surrounded by a wonderful light field called the aura or auric field. The aura is the light field that surrounds and holds together the matter of your embodiment. Through the means of Kirlian photography, your scientists have already photographed the first coronal field of the aura. Yet there are still greater electromagnetic fields that surround your body, for the aura extends from the density of electricity — the blue corona that surrounds the body — into the infiniteness of thought.

The aura is the Spirit of your being. The Spirit of your being — what I call the God of your being — connects directly to the mind of God, the flow of consciousness where all things are known. One part of the aura is a powerful, electromagnetic field of positive and negative electrum. Beyond the electromagnetic field, there are no divisions to the electrum. It is an undivided light sphere, which is pure energy. The light sphere allows all thought from the river of knowingness to flow through this great and powerful field. Which thoughts become known to you are determined by your thought processes, for the electromagnetic portion of your aura draws thought to you according to your thinking.

Your Spirit is like a sieve on the bank of the ever-moving, ever-changing river of thought. Through that light you stand in receivership of the mind of God, the thought flow where all knowledge is. Thus you have the ability to know all there is to know, for you are in the continuous flow of all consciousness, the river of all knowledge.

Consciousness is like a river, and your whole self — including every cell of your body — is continuously being fed by it, for thought supports and gives credence to your life. You live by thought from consciousness flow. Just as your body lives by the flow of blood that carries the substance of food to every cell, so is your whole self being sustained through the substance of thought emanating from the flow of consciousness.

You create every moment of your existence with thought that comes from consciousness flow. You are continuously taking thought from the river of thought, feeling it in your soul, feeding and expanding your entire being through that emotion, and putting the thought of your expanded self back out into the river, which expands the consciousness of all life. You may contemplate a thought of creativity this day and, as you do, the thought is felt, recorded in your soul as an electrical frequency, and that same frequency leaves your body and goes out into consciousness for someone else to pick up and create from. What you think and feel, everyone else has access to. They feed from your thoughts and you feed from theirs.

Consciousness consists of all thoughts emanating from all entities and all things. The thoughts that make up consciousness are of different electrical frequencies. Some are very low or slow frequency thoughts, those which predominate here in social consciousness. Others are higher frequency thoughts, the more unlimited thoughts of superconsciousness. Consciousness is the sum of all the different frequency values of thought, with each thought value attracting like values from everywhere.

Social consciousness is a density of electrical thought frequencies, yet one that is lighter than air. The density of social consciousness is constituted of expressed thought, thought that has been expressed through emotion by every entity; that is, it is made up of realized thought, thought that each entity has already taken in, felt in his soul, and distributed through his auric field back into the river of thought for everyone else to feed from.

The thoughts upon which your plane thrives are the limited, low frequency thoughts of social consciousness. Those thoughts are very restrictive, very judgmental, very harsh, because your lives are governed by attitudes related to survival and the fear of death, whether it is the death of the embodiment or the death of the ego. Thus your consciousness is occupied with thoughts of food, shelter, labor, gold; with judgments of proper and improper, good and bad; with fashion, beauty, acceptance, comparison, age, disease, and death. These low frequency thoughts easily come through your auric field because they predominate in the thinking of those around you. So you are continuously being fed by limited thoughts from a very restrictive, stagnated consciousness. And as you allow these thoughts to feed you, you put the feeling of them back out to regenerate and perpetuate the limited thinking of man.

The consciousness in your great cities is particularly limited because most of those who live there are very competitive, very time-and fashion-oriented, and very fearful and unaccepting of one another. Thus all of your great cities are enveloped by a thick density of consciousness. What those who come here from other universes see when they look upon your cities is a dense network of multicolored lights, low frequency thoughts of a very limited consciousness displayed as a light field.

The higher frequency thoughts of superconsciousness are those of Isness, being, life, harmony, oneness, ongoingness. They are the thoughts of love. They are the thoughts of joy. They are the thoughts of genius. They are the unlimited thoughts that are, in truth, beyond expression even through these words, for the feelings from unlimited thoughts go beyond words of description.

The higher frequency thoughts can be more easily experienced in the consciousness of the wilderness, away from the stagnated thinking of man, because there, life is simple, timeless, ongoing, and in complete harmony with itself. There, away from the judgment of man, you can hear the heartbeat of your own knowingness.

How do you have the ability to pick up thought from consciousness flow? The electromagnetic portion of your aura draws thought to you according to your thought processes and your emotional state of being. In order for thought to feed you — in order for it to be felt and realized within your being — it first must be lowered into a light form. Once thought meets the Spirit of your being , the light surrounding your body, it explodes into a burst of light; that is, thought ignites itself once it meets light. Light lowers the substance of thought; thus light has drawn like to it. Thought is unseen and then seen through a burst of light. The thought, in the form of light, enters your brain and is transmuted into an electrical light propellant of a given frequency, according to the value of the thought being received.

The moment you become aware of any one thing, you are receiving the thought of it. At the moment you are receiving the thought, the light of that thought is received by your brain. There are entities who occasionally see bursts of light, usually out of the sides of their eyes. What they are seeing in most instances is their own Spirit's acceptance of thought. The very moment they see the light before them in brilliant display is the moment that thought has entered into their auric field and displayed itself within their brain. If you close your eyes and see the movement of color or the expansion of designs, you are perceiving what thought looks like entering into your brain.

Your brain is a grand receiver of electrical thought frequencies, with different parts designed to receive, house, and amplify the different frequencies of thought. The different parts have different potentials to house and electrify thought, depending upon the density of water in its cellular walls. Some parts are capable of housing and amplifying only the higher thought frequencies; other parts house and amplify only the lower frequencies of thought.

Your brain does not create thought, contrary to popular belief. It simply allows thought to enter into it from consciousness flow. It is an organ designed by the Gods specifically for the purpose of receiving and housing thought that has come through the Spirit of your being, transforming it into an electrical current, amplifying it, and sending it through the central nervous system to every part of your body so that it can be realized for an understanding.

In your technology, you have what is termed radio receivers with gauges to determine sound volume and which megahertz or frequency level is received. Well, the brain is also a receiver with gauges, and it can receive a given frequency only if the part of your brain designed to house that frequency has been activated.

Your brain's ability to receive different thought frequencies is controlled by a powerful gauge called the pituitary gland, which is lodged between the left and right hemispheres of your brain. The pituitary, also called the seventh seal, rules your brain. It is responsible for activating different parts of your brain to receive and house the different thought frequencies. It is the door that opens your capacity to contemplate and reason with thought, realize it throughout your body, and manifest it into an experience for greater understanding.

The pituitary is a very small but very wonderful little gland that many call the third eye. Well, one does not have a third eye; there is no room for it in your head. The pituitary doesn't even look like an eye; it looks like a pear with a little mouth at the narrow point, and it appears to be petallike. Your brain is governed and controlled by the functions of this powerful gland through a complex system of hormone flows. The pituitary, which is a ductless gland, secretes a hormone that flows through the brain into the mouth of the pineal, another ductless gland, which sits near the pituitary at the base of the lower cerebrum and above the spinal column. The pineal, or sixth seal, is the gauge responsible for amplifying thought frequencies so they can be sent throughout the body. The hormone flow from the pituitary into the pineal is what activates different parts of your brain to receive and house the different thought frequencies.

The functions of the body are maintained in a harmony through the flow of hormones coming from ductless glands and issuing into the blood supply. The pineal is responsible for maintaining that harmony. The flow of hormones from the pineal activates all the other glands to secrete their hormones in harmony with each other, thus creating what is termed hormone balance. The level of that balance is determined by the collective thought frequencies being received by the pineal system. The higher the thought frequencies, the greater the hormone flow throughout the embodiment. Also, the greater the frequencies, the more the pineal activates the pituitary to secrete its hormone flow, which activates the brain to receive even higher thought frequencies.

How is thought from consciousness flow realized within your being? When thought comes through your aura, the aura does not define it, meaning it does not judge or alter the thought;

it lets it come forth unlimited. When thought propellants reach the brain, they travel first to the upper left hemisphere of the cerebrum, where the intellect or reasoning functions reside and the altered ego is expressed.

Now what is the altered ego? It is the understanding gained from the human experience that is stored in the soul and articulated through the reasoning portions of the brain. It is the collective attitudes of God/man living merely as a surviving creature, living in the shadow of social consciousness. And that collective view will refuse to accept any thought frequency that does not fit within its security, that does not help to insure the survival of the entity. The altered ego is the refusal to allow all thoughts to be received and entertained for a greater realization within the embodiment.

Each thought frequency that the altered ego allows to flow into the brain is transferred into an electrical current and sent to that portion of the brain that has been activated by the pituitary to house that frequency. That portion of the brain then amplifies the current and sends it to the pineal system.

The pineal system governs your central nervous system. It collects each frequency of thought given to it, further amplifies it, and propels it through the central nervous system, which runs through the spinal column as a highway of electrical thought. The electrical current coming from the pineal system flows through the fluid of the central nervous system — which is water — down through the spine and then through every nerve to every cell of your body.

Now every cell in your body is fed through the blood supply with gas derived from the action of enzymes on food intake. When the electrical current from the thought enters into the cellular structures, it enters as a spark of light. The spark ignites the cell, causing the gas to expand, which allows the cell to duplicate itself in what is called a cloning process, allows it to create another cell and to regenerate itself. Thus the whole of the body is fed through that one singular thought. That is how life is substantiated within the molecular structures of the embodiment, through the effects of all the thoughts that you allow yourself to receive every moment of your existence.

As thought continuously feeds every cell of your body, your entire body responds to its electrical impulse — your entire body. Thus the effect of thought, experienced throughout every cell, creates a feeling, a sensation, an emotion, or what is termed a rush within the body. That feeling is then sent to your soul to be recorded there.

Your soul is a grand recorder, an unbiased computer which records very scientifically every emotion felt within your embodiment. When you feel emotional, you are feeling a thought that has bombarded the light structure of your being, has been accepted through your brain, and has been sent throughout the central nervous system to produce a sensation in every cell of your body. The soul then records that sensation as an emotion for the purpose of referral, what is termed memory.

Memory does not have size; it is an essence. Memory is not a visual accounting; it is an emotional accounting. It is emotion that creates the visual image. The soul does not record pictures or words for the purpose of memory; it records the emotions of those images and words.

The soul takes the emotion created by thought being felt throughout the body and searches through its memory banks for a resemblance, one which the reasoning portions of the brain — what you term intellect — can identify in order to select a word to describe the feeling.

Everything you can describe has certain feelings associated with it, based on experience. You know flowers as flowers because of your emotional experiences with them. You have seen and touched and smelled and worn the structures called flowers. Thus the flower feels a certain way to you. You know silk as silk because you associate with it certain sensations and emotional experiences, which give rise to the understanding termed silk. The soul has recorded all of that information from your emotional experiences. So when the feeling from the thought is felt, the soul records that feeling and searches its memory banks for similar feelings from prior thoughts experienced. It then sends that information back to your brain to indicate that the thought has been realized, understood in its totality throughout the embodiment. Thought is not realized simply through your brain; it is realized in the totality of your body. The reasoning portion of your brain then allows you to formulate a word to describe the feeling.

How is thought realized and known? Through emotion. Knowingness is wholly a feeling. The thought of anything cannot be known until it is first felt; then it has an identity. To know a thought is to accept it into your brain and then allow yourself to feel it, to experience it throughout your body. Knowledge is not the proving of any one thing; it is the emotional ascertainment of it. Once you have the feeling within, then you can say, "I know. I have the feeling. I know."

Within you indeed, my beloved masters, lies the door to all knowledge. The fire that burns within you is the same fire that flickers in every minute atom, in every great star, in every cellular form, in everything that is. It is the same identical fire. Your oneness with all life is realized through the principle of light, for the light that gives credence to emotion in your soul is the same light that gives life to the blossoms, the stars, and to everything else that is. So within you, you possess the ability to know all things. To know anything is not to understand it through intellectual rhetoric that is surrounded with elaborate words that mean nothing. The knowingness of the flower is reached by the inner being through feelings. You can always tell how something is thinking through the frequency it emits called emotion. If you want to know anything, all you have to do is feel it. You will always be absolutely correct.

How does thought create the experiences of your life? The pineal is the seal of knowing into manifestation. Whatever knowingness you allow yourself to receive will become a reality first in your body, for the pineal is responsible for sending that thought as an electrical current throughout your body, to be registered as emotion. The more unlimited the thought, the greater and faster the frequency that is shot throughout your body; thus the greater the high or rush experienced in your body. That feeling is then recorded and stored in your soul as a given frequency.

The feeling of every thought, recorded in your soul, is then put forth into your aura as an expectancy, and that expectancy activates the electromagnetic portion of your light field to draw to you — much like a magnet — the likeness of whatever your collective-attitude thinking is. It will draw to you situations, things, objects, or entities that will create the same feelings experienced in your body from all of your thoughts. Why? So you can experience your thoughts through a three-dimensional reality for the prize of experience called wisdom.

How are your desires manifested? A desire is nothing more than the thought of fulfillment seen through an object, entity, or experience. Whatever thought of fulfillment you allow yourself to feel leaves your body through your electromagnetic field, and it goes into consciousness flow to draw to you whatever will produce the same feeling from the desire experienced in your body. The more completely and intensely that desire is felt within your body, the more complete will be its fulfillment. And the more you know with absolute certainty that your desire will be fulfilled, the quicker the manifestation, for absolute knowingness is a high-frequency thought that enhances the expectancy put forth through the auric field, thus amplifying your power to manifest your desires.

You have the ability to know everything there is to know. That is what your brain was designed for, so that a God living on a physical plane in a physical body could experience and understand whatever dimension of God he desired, seen through three-dimensional forms. Whatever thoughts you allow yourself to know through your wonderful receiver will become an experienced reality, seen first within your embodiment and then through the conditions of your life. And whatever you desire, you have the ability — through knowing — to manifest into your life in the twinkling of an eye. That is how you create the kingdom of heaven on earth.

It is a simple science. Remember: Thought is; then light is seen; then light is lowered into electrical impulses. Electrical impulses are lowered, lowered, lowered to become mass, and from the mass they are lowered to represent the thought ideal.

The same truth works in the body. It is thought, light, receiving unit; from the receiving unit, it takes the electrum and runs it through the mass in order for the mass to understand through feeling. To manifest your desires, all you have to do is feel whatever you desire, and the feeling is sent back to the Father to fulfill your desires. That is all there is to it. Too simple? You want it more complex?

***

CHAPTER 18

The Closed Mind

The whole of your brain capacity is immense, yet you in your limited thinking use only one-third of it. What do you think the rest is for, to fill up an empty hole?

Though your brain was designed to receive every frequency of thought in the mind of God, in the entirety of knowingness it will be activated to receive only those frequencies you allow yourself to receive. And of all the wonderful thoughts bombarding the God that holds you together, the only knowingness that most allow is of the lower frequency thoughts of social consciousness, which are very limited, very cloistered, as you have well experienced. And when you live according to social consciousness and reason only with the frequencies that predominate in its limited thinking, the only parts of your brain that are activated are the upper left and right levels of the cerebrum and portions of the lower cerebellum, which sits upon your spinal column. The majority of your brain remains dormant; it does nothing. That is because any thought that does not fit in with the limited thinking of your family, peers, society, or dogma, you will refute. You will turn it away, meaning you allow yourself to contemplate and reason only with those thoughts which will be accepted by others.

You have a term called closed-minded. Well, that is a literal description. When you refuse to venture in thought beyond the bounds of social consciousness, portions of your brain are literally closed to the higher frequencies of thought. That is because your pituitary gland has been activated to open its mouth only a little way; thus it has activated into use only those parts of the brain that receive the lower frequencies of social consciousness.

The only reason someone is a genius and knows things you do not know is because he has opened his mind to contemplate the what-ifs, the outrageous thoughts, the thoughts of brilliance that go beyond the limited thinking of man. He has allowed himself to entertain and reason with these thoughts, whereas you have rejected them. You cannot receive them because you have yet to activate those portions of your brain that will enable you to reason with them. So what happens to the great thoughts of unlimited understanding that continually bombard your light structure? They bounce off your receiver unit and are sent back out through the Spirit of your being, back into the river of thought.

To be closed-minded is to be closed to the possibility of anything existing outside of the values that can be experienced through the senses of your body. Yet in the realm called God, nothing is impossible. If any one thing can be conceived or pondered, it exists, for whatever is dreamed or imagined is already within the realm of existence. That is how all of creation came into being. Anytime you tell someone that something is only your imagination, you are programming them into stupidity and limited creativity. And that is indeed what happens to the children on this plane — all of you.

I tell you, whatever is allowed to be thought of, is. And whatever you allow yourself to think, you will experience, for your electromagnetic field will draw it to you.

You know, the atrocity of being closed-minded is that it keeps you from knowing joy. It keeps you enslaved to the illusions of man. It keeps you from knowing the glory of yourself and God. As long as you have a cloistered mind and live and think according to social consciousness, you will never venture into the unknown or contemplate the possibility of greater realities for fear that it will mean change. And certainly it will, because there will be more to see, to understand, and to be a part of, than there was before in a tidy world that lives and dies. As long as you accept only those limited thoughts that have been bred into you, you will never activate greater portions of your brain to receive and experience any thought other than what you have faced every day of your existence.

Each time you accept a thought that is greater than what you have accepted as your standard, that thought activates yet another part of your brain into purposeful use. Each time you do that, the greater thought will offer itself as a carrier to expand your reasoning from that point. That will activate other portions of your brain for more thought, for more receiving, for more knowing. When you desire to experience superconsciousness, unlimited thinking, your pituitary begins to open and bloom like a magnificent flower. The more it opens, the greater the hormone flow and the more the dormant parts of your brain are activated to receive the higher frequencies of thought.

You know, it is very simple to be a genius. All you have to do is think for yourself.

The brain has been a great mystery that has perplexed many. They take it out to look at it and they can't find anything in it, save its fluids, which are water. Water is a conductor of electrical current. The denser the water, the greater the amplification of the electrical current put through it. In the dormant portions of your brain, the fluid is denser for the purpose of amplifying the higher thought frequencies into greater electrical currents and sending them throughout the body at a greater rate of speed. So when you allow more of your thoughts to be housed in the dormant parts, your body is activated to become quicker and more profound in its responses. You can do anything with your body once the totality of your brain is in use. Through your soul — which is recording and holding steadfast the emotion of every thought you receive — your brain and its impulses to your body can create your body to be however your thoughts determine it to be.

Do you know that if your brain were used to its full capacity, you could change your body into a wisp of light in a moment and your body would live forever? Do you know that your brain has the ability to grow a new limb if you are missing one? Fully operational, your brain has the ability to completely heal your body in a splendid moment, or to change it physically into any ideal you give it.

The whole of your brain capacity is immense, yet you in your limited thinking have been able to use only one-third of it. What do you think the rest of it is for, to fill up an empty hole?

Your body is maintained according to your brain and your collective thinking, for every thought you allow to enter your brain electrifies and feeds every cell of your body. Yet from the time you were a child and could reason in social consciousness, you accepted the programming that you must grow up, become old, and then die. So because you accepted that thought, you began to degrade the life force within your body, because the thought of olderness sends a slow or low frequency, electrical spark to each cellular structure. The slower the rate of speed, the greater the loss of agility within the body, for the body is lessened in its ability to rejuvenate and restore itself. Thus age is permitted to occur and ultimately the death of the body. Yet if you allowed yourself to continuously receive higher thought frequencies, you would send faster and more high-powered electrical currents throughout your body and it would stay forever in the moment, thus never advancing in age or dying. But everyone here knows it will age and die, so slowly the current becomes less and less and less.

Those portions of your brain that have not been activated at the present have the ability — simply through knowing — to reconstruct any damaged part within your body, wherever it is. The moment you know your body can heal itself, that thought sends a greater spark through the central nervous system to where the damaged part is, which will cause the DNA factor within each cell to clone and reconstruct the cell perfectly. Perfectly. You think that is miraculous? That is the way it should be and is.

You think that the only way your body can be healed is through physicians and medicines. And they work, for you believe that they do. You have also been told — and believe — that you cannot do it on your own; thus you cannot, for that knowingness is present. Yet there are entities who have sought out healers, knowing that what they would hear would be an absolute truth. And by knowing it, it became an absolute truth within the embodiment; thus they were healed in a moment. That is what knowingness does, and it can change your body to however you want it to be. You have the capacity to be unlimited even in your bodily movement, for it was designed to be that way.

Every moment of your existence — whether you are asleep or awake, whether you are conscious or unconscious — you are continuously receiving thought from the mind of God. And whatever thought frequencies you allow to come through this wonderful God that holds you together, you will experience for the prize and the only reality of life called emotion. So you who are feeling unhappy, dull, morose, fearful, bitter, angry, jealous, hurried, unloved, unwanted, what thought frequencies are you allowing yourself to feel? Social consciousness. Where is joy, you ask? Where is love? Where is forever? Where is God? Only a thought away.

Why don't you know all of these wonderful thoughts that pass through your Spirit every moment? You haven't wanted to know them. You have chosen to live in the shadow of social consciousness, to dress and act and think like the herd. You have chosen to fit in, to be accepted, so that you could survive. You didn't want to know because to entertain the thoughts that you are a sovereign, that you are God, that you are forever, that you are all-knowing, would mean going against the grain of your family, your friends, your religion, and your country. So you gave away your power. You gave up your sovereignty. You forgot your identity. You closed down your brain. To teach you how to open it back up is the reason I am here.

What is this religious figure called God, that infinite mystery that man has desperately searched to find for eons? It is thought and its ability to receive itself and, by receiving itself, to become and expand itself. That is all God is: the totality of thought, the eminence of life. And right within your own being you have the power to become God completely — completely — for if the full spectrum of your brain were in use, you would be this moment to the ends of forever; you would know all that is known; you would be the hue of the sun, the depths of the sea, the power of the wind, and the star upon the horizon.

What keeps you from knowing and becoming the totality of God? Altered ego, because altered ego cuts God off by refusing to accept all the thought frequencies that God is so it can live safe and secure, out of harm's way. That is why the altered ego is indeed what is termed the antichrist, because it denies that you are the son of God. It does not allow you to accept the thought and to realize that you and the Father are one and the same, that you are the divine and immortal principle that has the power to create forever and the power to create death.

The antichrist is the altered ego and its kingdom is social consciousness. It is that which does not allow unlimited thought; and its dogma is fear, judgment, and survival. The Christ is man wholly expressing the power, the beauty, the love, and unlimited life of the Father that lives within him. It is man realizing that he is divine and becoming that realization, transcending dogma, prophesy, and fear, for he knows that beyond social consciousness lies the unlimited vigor called God.

So the antichrist and the Christ share the same temple, and that temple is you. Everything is within you because the God that you are allows both the antichrist and the Christ to be. It allows life and death. It allows limitation and unlimitedness.

You have heard of the prophesy called Armageddon? Well, you have been living it all of this life. Armageddon is the battle between the realization of God and the recognition of the antichrist, which is the altered ego that does not allow unlimited thoughts to enter your brain for unlimited expression. It is the war between social consciousness and unlimited knowingness. That is Armageddon — not a battle outside of you, but inside — the conflict within you between the Christ arising and the altered ego staying in control. Hence, the prophesy is indeed coming to pass in these times.

To be God is to be unlimited knowingness, unlimited being. To be man is to be the limited creature who does not open his mind for greater knowledge, who accepts theory and does not practice living, who is the taught rather than the teacher, the protected rather than the explorer.

I tell you, you have the ability to know everything there is to know. And you also possess the ability to manifest everything you ever want. You also possess the ability to live forever in your body, if that is your desire. But to all these things, the altered ego says, "Nay." So for that you will know who man is, but God will always remain a mystery.

***

CHAPTER 19

Opening The Mind

The more you love yourself, the more your brain is opened up. Then you become more than your body. You become that which holds you together.

All of you have grown to your capacity in your learning of God in the limited form of matter. Through all of your many lives upon this plane, you have experienced all the elements of this paradise of your own remarkable creativity. And through that experience you have learned all there is to know of the limited thought values of God/man living in the herdlike reality of social consciousness. You have already learned of fear and insecurity, of sorrow, anger, greed. You have already learned of jealousy, hatred, war. You have already learned of death. You have indeed already learned of the alienation of yourself from your divine Source, which has loved and supported you throughout all your adventures in order for you to experience God in the last level of its spectacular display of Isness.

In order to return to a state of unlimitedness, to experience joy and the freedom of being, you must once again become that which holds you together. And the only way to become that — since you are encumbered with a body — is to fully activate your seventh seal, pituitary, so that your brain can receive the unlimited thoughts that lie just beyond social consciousness. That is how you expand your knowingness into the unlimited understanding of God, that which allows and loves and is the totality of itself, which is the totality of thought.

So how do you get this wonderful little gland to awaken the dormant portions of your brain through its hormone flow? Simply through desire. To become a Christ is to desire to know the Father and become the likeness of God. It is the desire to allow all thought to become the reality of self. It is the desire to love in every moment all that you have become. It is the desire to be the Isness of all that you are.

Why is it important to love the totality of what you are? When you do, you immediately transcend social consciousness. Then you rise above acceptance. You transcend judgment. You go beyond the illusion of time. Then you live only for the fulfillment of self. You listen only to the voice within. You follow only the path of joy. And on that path lies the knowingness of all that is.

Now you say to me, "But, Ramtha, that is being wholly selfish." Indeed it is. But selfish is Godish. Every moment you live for the love of this God within you — every illusion you embrace and give up, everything you do to find your joy and light — emanates from your being into consciousness flow to feed the whole of mankind. When you live wholly for the love of self — which is the love of God — then you exude God into the density of social consciousness. Then you light the way for your beloved brothers on their own paths back into self, the only path that will take them home to their beloved Father.

When you love yourself enough to feel worthy to receive all that God is and you desire to know that you are one with the Father, then you begin to bloom this wondrous flower. That is how you open the capacity of your brain to receive all thought values in the mind of God: by wanting to know, by desiring to feel all the emotion of that knowingness.

What is the greatest way to manifest any desire? By speaking it forth from the Lord God of your being. The lord of your being, which is your soul, governs your body through its emotional structure. It is from the soul that your pituitary is instructed to release its hormone flow. The God of your being is the light that encompasses all that you are and allows all thoughts to come into your being. The being is the ego that is experiencing the realities of matter through the bodily form, which is what encourages judgment and alters the Isness or purity of thought; hence the term altered ego. So when you speak from the Lord God of your being, you are bringing into alignment the totality of what you are, which gives you the greatest power to manifest and create whatever you want.

When you desire from the Lord God of your being to receive unlimited thoughts, that thought of fulfillment felt within your soul manifests in your body to activate the pituitary gland, and it begins to open. As it begins to open, a greater hormone flow goes through the pineal gland and, as it does, it awakens the dormant mind. It opens another part of your brain to allow greater and more refined frequencies of thought to be experienced throughout your body.

When thoughts of a greater frequency come in, they are taken through the awakened portion of your brain. The pineal gland in the back of your head receives the greater frequency and it begins to swell, which causes your head to ache, or you may feel a little dizzy or lightheaded. That frequency is then turned into a high-powered electrical current and shot through your central nervous system to every cell of your body. From that you will feel a rush, or sensations of tingling, of being lifted, because greater energy than you have felt before is now rushing throughout your body. That frequency ignites every cell, causing it to increase its vibrational frequency. The more you receive unlimited thoughts, the greater the body vibrates. And you begin to take on a glow because you are beginning to reverse the body from density back into light.

How will you describe the feeling of unlimited thoughts? You cannot. The knowingness of an unlimited thought has no word that you can associate with it because it is a new thought being experienced, a new emotion, an immense feeling that moves you in a profound yet quiet manner. Knowingness will come to you as pure feeling: unannounced, unidentified, nameless emotion.

Most who seek enlightenment think that it will come in the form of words. But if what you understand can be described by words, you have felt it all before. If it can't, and you are simply feeling, what you are feeling is genius; it is brilliance; it is indeed unlimited thinking. All the things you have wanted to understand do not have words; they have emotion and vision. And when the knowingness comes, you will be speechless with feelings.

The art of limiting thought is associating words with it. A master explains nothing; he only knows it. To explain it means he must limit himself. When you get to the point that you simply know — without having to justify or explain your knowingness — then you are indeed the master of your kingdom. Then you are in absolute knowingness.

What happens to the feeling of upliftment experienced from higher frequency thoughts? It is captivated in your soul, which forever holds it there in memory. Your soul permits the memory of unlimited thoughts to occur through emotion, feeling. Thus it captivates your knowingness for all times, so that what you have allowed yourself to receive can be reached over and over again.

The other wonderful thing that happens to that feeling of upliftment is that your soul emanates it through your auric field into consciousness flow, which not only lifts the density of consciousness but draws into your life a situation that will produce the same feeling. Why? So the thought can be completely understood through experience. When the higher frequency thought is thoroughly understood, it is recorded in your soul as wisdom. The wisdom means that the knowingness has become solidified within you as an absolute. The wisdom not only elevates the frequency level of the soul — which will cause your life to conform to its greater emotional being — but it also further activates the pituitary to allow the brain to receive and reason with even greater, higher frequency thoughts, and on and on and on.

As your pituitary begins to flower, things change in your life in ways you would never have thought possible. Everything you think, you feel with great emotion. As the knowingness you feel inside works its way into a creative form, you begin to see your thoughts manifesting quicker and quicker. Your love, understanding, and compassion are enhanced. And entities fall away from your life because you have risen to a different understanding. Yet in their place, others of like thinking are drawn to you.

Soon, as brilliance, creativity, and knowingness intensify within you, you begin to know and feel things that you haven't felt or known before. You are able to look upon another entity and feel that entity within your being. From your thoughts, you are able to know of your days to come.

You think a psychic is a rare entity? That is only because you think like social consciousness, and social consciousness does not think that those great abilities could be really rather normal. Everyone is psychic. When you allow yourself to know, you know everything, for knowingness — uninhibited by the illusions of social consciousness — removes the veil from your eyes so that you can see other dimensions. It removes the blocks from your ears so you can hear the music of all life vibrating in harmony with itself. And how do you make it happen? By desiring it.

The more you desire unlimitedness and the more you embrace and feel the thoughts that come forth, the more the pituitary secretes its hormone and the wider its mouth becomes. The more you desire to love what you are and to live in knowingness, the more your brain is opened up by the God that surrounds your being, greater and greater and greater. Then you become more than your body. You become that which holds you together.

The pituitary is indeed the door to God. The more you allow unlimited thoughts into your brain, the more it opens. The more it opens, the more you will know. And whatever you know, you will become.

The flower is emanating a thought frequency. At the same moment the rug is emanating a thought frequency. When you have the ability to pick up all thought frequencies, you can become whatever finished frequency you choose. Then you have the absolute freedom to become the wind or anything else that you wish.

Soon the whole of the pituitary system is in full bloom

and the whole of your brain is activated. Then all that the pituitary has had within its spiritual embodiment is given to the full mind, and the mind can never go back to a limited state. Once the flower begins to open, it never closes again; it is open for all times.

When your brain is completely activated, your point in reality becomes vacillating. That is why though you are here, you can be on the seventh level; though you are on the seventh level, you can be in the Pleiades; though you are in the Pleiades, you can be at a friend's side.

When your pituitary is in full bloom, you cease to die; you cease to grow old. Whatever you tell your body to do, it will do. You can tell the body to quicken its vibratory frequency and it will elevate itself into another dimension. That is how powerful your brain is. You can even resurrect your body from the dead. When you are that powerful, you are wearing the divine crown of God. And when you are pure God, which is pure life, then you are forever. Then you are everything. That is the grandest heaven.

So the great seventh seal has crowned itself, and the whole of your mind is awakened and the whole embrace of knowingness is allowed through your beautiful receiver. The more you know and the more your body experiences that frequency, the faster the body vibrates until it becomes lighter and lighter and lighter. Then one day when all life you have loved and embraced — and the soul is complete in the experiences here — that same knowingness and that same vibration will increase itself a millionfold, and it will take the body into invisibility and away from this place. Then you are off the wheel of life after life.

You are a creature of three dimensions — Spirit, soul, and ego — expressing on a plane of density. And only with three dimensions can you realize forever. Address the Lord God of your being. It will hear you. When you do, it is a lord, a God, a master who speaks. When you tell it to remember, it will remember. When you tell it to be greater, it will be greater. And when you desire from the Lord God of your being to possess unlimited understanding, it will open up your mind to allow greater frequencies of thought to be felt in the body for knowingness. That is all you have to do. That is commanding it to do so, and the ductless glands obey. And when feelings come forth that electrify your being into a greater understanding, give thanks to the God within you for it being so simple.

How can you be more understanding of all that is? Know that you are. How you think and speak determines how much you allow yourself to know. Do not say, "I hope to know more," for then you never will. And do not say, "I will try to know more," for trying has never accomplished. And do not say, "I seek to know more," for seeking never finds. Say, "From the Lord God of my being, I now know all there is to know in this moment. So be it," and await the answers. Whether or not you realize at that moment what you desire to know, saying "I know" opens the door for that realization to occur. That is all you have to say, and the knowledge will come forth.

How you limit your creativity and your life is by saying you do not know or by doubting the knowingness that comes to you. The worst abomination is the phrase, "I don't know." Remember, you are the lawgiver, and what you think and then speak is the law. If you say, "I don't know," you won't. If you say, "I can never," you never will. If you say, "I am not worthy of my Father's love," you will never receive it. If you speak this way, it means you must think this way. And if you think this way, the feeling of that thought registers in your soul, and your soul manifests the reality that fulfills your thought processes.

You are like a computer. Each day you compute into your knowledge, doubts. You compute into your knowledge, lacking. You compute into your knowledge, indeed, not knowing. You are the robber of your own kingdom, for you who know only doubt and limitation have robbed the very life force from yourself by how you think and speak.

I tell you, you have the ability to know all there is and ever will be. The door that opens you up to that knowledge is simply to say, "I know," and the realization of it will soon follow. It may be moments or days, but it will come. It always does, for the word "knowing" is absolute, and it brings your desire into absoluteness. The thought of knowing, felt within your soul, manifests within your being to open your pituitary to permit greater thoughts to be received. Knowing is the door that allows the river of thought to flow into you in an unlimited flow.

Now knowingness is not belief. Belief is conjectural; knowingness is absolute. The only thing that brings on knowingness is knowing. When you believe in something, the soul understands the word believe to really mean that someone — or even your own self — is assailing you to convince you of a truth that you have no awareness or certainty of, for that truth has not become an experienced reality.

I do not ask you to believe in anything. I want you to know. To be enlightened is to know, without doubt, belief, faith, or hope. All of those things are conjectural. As long as you believe or have faith in anything, it never will be. Knowing makes it absolute, which brings what is known into manifestation. Through the manifestation of the realized thought into an experience, the understanding will occur to you. Then it is a part of your being and not something you must convince yourself of.

Absolute knowing is the creator of the whole of your kingdom. To be in all-knowingness, simply say, "I know." Don't ever doubt or be hesitant. Know, absolutely. Every moment you say, "I know," that is a thought of certainty felt within your being, which permits the space for that knowingness to occur. Genius occurs when you open the door of knowingness so that greater thoughts can come forth into a creative form.

If you will say steadfastly, "From the Lord God of my being, I now know the answer to this and am in a state of receivership for it. So be it," that calls forth the knowingness into a resolve. Though the realization may not be there at the moment, the door stands wide open for it to be realized in an experience from which wisdom will be gained. Your being will quickly adjust itself to become what the knowingness now is. You do not have to work toward that accomplishment. You do not have to strive or search or struggle for it. You do not have to go through chants or rituals to obtain it. Simply know. By knowing, you are in a state of receivership for the awareness of it.

How do you quicken the manifestation of your desires? By knowing. Knowing is the door that allows the kingdom of heaven to display its abundance within the kingdom of self. Knowing that a desire — whatever it is — is already fulfilled, amplifies the thought of your desire, sends it through your auric field into consciousness flow, and manifests your desire so that you may stand in receivership of its completion.

The truth is, all things are already yours. When you know they are, then they are made available to you. You must understand that the principal giver of all that you need is you and your ability to receive what you want. The way to receive your desires is simply to know what you want and know you are worthy of getting it. Knowingness is the truth; it is the giver; it is your future. When you speak, know it is. Whatever you want, you may have by simply knowing that you are the lawgiver and that whatever you know and speak must be. That is called the Law of One.

I tell you, you know all there is to know and you may have all you desire. In this moment of knowing, you simply have not realized that truth. Knowing opens the door to that realization. It activates another part of your brain so the thought can become a manifested reality. Then when the experience of your unlimited thinking has indeed come to pass, that solidifies in the ego part of your brain the realization that knowing does work, which gives you the strength to go a step further into even more unlimited thinking.

If I could take all of your words away and give you but a sparse few, they would be: I now know. I am absolute. I am complete. I am God. I Am. If there were no other words but those, you would no longer be limited to this plane.

How much greater is it for you to know than to assume or believe? How much greater is it for you to know than to be a maybe? How much greater is it for you to know than not to know? It takes the same thought processes, the same energy, the same facial expression and bodily movement to know as it does to not know.

Know. Simply know. "I know this will occur. I know I

am God. I know I am happy. I know I am." Know, know, know. That is all it takes. Always know. If you say you don't or you can't, you never will. Say you now know. Then you will know everything.

Do you know the difference between you and me? I know I am an unlimited God, and you don't. That is the only difference. I know I am, and you have yet to realize you are. Your society says you aren't, but what do they know? They bury themselves every day.

Why have you obstructed your knowingness? Because in your endeavor to understand thought in the form called matter, your thought processes became so caught up in the realities of matter that you altered your whole perception of life. You see, matter is a level of thought that is created by altering thought to its greatest extent. It is created by lowering thought into light, into electrum, and then dividing the electrum into parts that have negative and positive values. So every time you relate to God in the form of matter, you are perceiving and understanding thought according to divisions or polarities rather than the purity and the undivided Isness that it is. The more you are focused in matter and oriented to survival, the more you see life in terms of polar dimensions: up/down, near/far, fast/slow, light/dark, big/little, hot/cold, good/bad, positive/negative.

To go back to the Isness of pure thought, you must master the altered ego, the reasoning portion of your brain that is oriented to living and surviving in matter. The altered ego is that which perceives according to the illusions of time, distance, and separateness. It is that which perceives in terms of survival and acceptance. It is that which divides and judges pure thought.

A pure thought can come to any of you, but quickly you ascertain whether it is right or wrong for you, should you or should you not do it, is it possible or impossible, real or imagined, reasonable or unreasonable. Every time you judge your thought by dividing it to where it has a positive and a negative, you have altered it into a lower frequency value. Knowingness does not judge anything. When you know, you never ponder if a thought is true or correct. All thoughts are true and correct. Knowing does not weigh or value thought. Knowing allows thought to be an Isness. It allows your thought processes to be without interruption or interception.

To see another plane, to hear a finer sound, to become lighter than your weight, all you need is to know that they are realities and allow that knowingness to be experienced in your body. That is all you have to do. If you do not believe they are real, not believing is a judgment that keeps your brain from becoming greater. Thus all of that knowingness that is coming through your Spirit every moment bounces off your brain and is sent back to the mind of the Father. Then all you will ever receive is what keeps you secure on this plane and limited to it.

When you desire from the Lord God of your being to possess unlimited knowingness, you must allow all thoughts to enter your brain consciousness — unaltered by judgments — so that they can be fully experienced in your body. Through that conscious allowing by the altered ego, which gives credence to your desire, the pituitary activates another part of your brain to receive unlimited understanding.

What has enabled you to receive a thought of creativity out of the blue when you wanted it? You merely allowed its entrance into your knowingness. That is all you did. It was there all along, waiting for you to ask for it and allow it to enter your receiver. That is all it takes. And the less your thought processes are caught up in judgments and altered thinking, the easier it is for the thoughts of superconsciousness to enter your brain receiving unit.

Learn to see yourself and life through the eyes of Isness. When you behold a flower, do not say it is ugly or beautiful. That is a judgment that has altered the thought of the flower. What is pure is the thought "flower." When you look at the flower and you see it as flower, light, life, Isness, then you are allowing yourself to receive the purity and the Isness of the thought, which sends a higher frequency electrum to be felt throughout your body. Then you think as a Christ thinks, for you see all things as an equality and an Isness. Each time you do not limit and judge your experiences, you permit your brain to be activated to receive the unlimited thoughts that go beyond your everyday existence.

Never judge the thoughts you receive. Do not think of something as being positive, for how could it be positive without saying that there is also negative? If you say, "This is good," that means that some things are bad. When you tender yourself, love yourself, do not say you are beautiful or lovely; say you are God. When you do something with your neighbor, do not say it is good; say it is God. That means that it is, that it is simply a pure and virtuous experience of life.

When you look upon other entities in the expression of their lives, never see them as other than an Isness. If you judge their expression as being good or bad, positive or negative, you create in yourself a perception of alteredness. And whatever you perceive, you will become, for that thought will register as a feeling within your being. Thus you victimize your own self because you — not they — experience the effects of your judgment. And that feeling recorded in your soul sets up a precedent by which you will continue to judge your own actions and your own being.

When you condemn another for something, you are only condemning aspects of yourself seen within them. That is why they are so easy to identify. That is why your attention is drawn to those aspects. The other entity has served merely as a mirror of your own inner judgments, a tool for you to reconcile judgments of yourself that you have accepted from others.

When you look upon others, see them as an Isness and in what is termed an evenness. If they are being cruel or hateful to another, to say they are cruel or hateful is a truth, for that is indeed how they are expressing. That is their experience of Isness. To say they are bad or wrong or evil in that expression is a judgment, which becomes wholly your experience, alteredness.

No one is worth judging. No color of skin, no action, no anything is worth altering yourself out of a state of God, of Isness. Whoever they are, however they are expressing, love them for the God within them that allows them to be that way. Simply by virtue of their being, they are to be loved. The fact that they exist is greater than anything they will ever do. Love them for being, for as long as they are, it is a certainty that you will be. If you love them regardless of who they are and let that love just be, then you will always be pure in your being.

Now what is the easiest way to remove judgments from your thought processes? By becoming aware of your feelings and the thoughts that gave birth to them. Simply through that awareness will you teach yourself to be more refined in your thinking.

When you feel unhappy, sad, angry, fearful, hurried, separate — or any other feeling that you do not like — examine your thinking. You will soon see the connection between your altered thinking — judging yourself or others, or seeing life in facets or dimensions — and your displeasing emotions. And soon, as you tire of these feelings, you will begin to refine your thinking to remove the judgments that separate you from life. As you do, and as you allow more and more unlimited thoughts to be experienced in your being, you will also begin to see a connection between your unlimited thinking and the feelings of peace, joy, harmony, and lightness in the bodily movement. And never judge yourself for issuing forth judgments. Have mercy on yourself and simply allow the awareness of your thoughts and feelings to teach you, for I assure you they will.

Of all the words ever created, there is one that most fits this teaching, and that is called being. Being. And what does that mean? It means allowing yourself to be however you are and wholly loving yourself for being that. It is feeling whatever you are feeling and living that emotion. Being is living wholly in the moment because you know that the Now is all there is. It is doing whatever you want to do, living the adventure that your soul urges you to pursue.

What is the reason for being? When you live that way, you never judge yourself or others or the thoughts that occur to you. Then there is neither right nor wrong, possible nor impossible, perfection nor imperfection, positive nor negative. There is no longer the illusion of time which does not permit you to feel and savor the beauty of the moment. When you are in a state of being, there is only the Isness of life and the ongoingness of the Now.

In a state of being, your thoughts no longer dally in the past or future, preoccupied with guilt and remorse, musts and shoulds. In being, you do not hold to any particular truth but are the reviewer of all truths. You see all truths as an Isness and allow each to be explored to determine if it is workable in your state of being. When you live that way, then all thoughts that come to you are pondered and, through your brain, understood in your body as feelings, which allows more knowing, more thought, more Isness to come forth.

When you simply are, you are in alignment with the Isness of all things. And through that alignment, you may have anything you desire, and you have to do nothing except be. The God of your being will draw to you whatever you think, whatever you desire, and it will come. Those who busy themselves by trying to do every outward principle make a little mockery of the inward one. In being, you already have and are everything.

When you simply are, and you allow yourself to receive all thoughts, then you can hear the voice of God. Then everything you ever wanted to know you may know in the twinkling of an eye. When you do not judge your thoughts but allow them to manifest as emotion within your soul, you are living as an unlimited God merely by being open to the Isness and all that it is. Then you become a pure channel of your own God-self and you come closer to the pure simplicity of the mind of God.

Learn to live by knowing and allowing. Then you have mastered the altered ego. Then you have mastered the seventh level, the seventh seal, the seventh heaven, for on the seventh there is no judgment; there is only the ongoing Isness of life. Once you have mastered judgment, you have mastered the totality of this plane and can leave whenever you desire.

Unless you have the ability in this moment to clone for yourself another body — which you are capable of doing when your brain is fully functional — don't be in such a hurry to destroy it.

Love your body. Be kind to it; nourish it; tender it. It is the pure instrument of expression that allows you to experience life on this plane. Become unlimited in your thought processes but also take care of the vehicle that allows you to do that.

If you are a woman, be a woman; if a man, be a man. Love what you are. Never abuse your body. Never deface or defile it. Do not make it do things it was not designed to do.

Look upon the grandeur of your being. Hold yourself divine. Clothe yourself in what is the finest against your skin. Anoint yourself. Perfume yourself. Feed yourself only what your body wants. If you listen to it, it will tell you what it needs in order to nourish itself.

Never put into your body that which is harmful, which you know is harmful. Anything that causes the lack of oxygen flow to your brain causes the cells to perish in great numbers and they will never be again, for the brain lacks the ability to reproduce its cells. When your brain cells are destroyed, then you lessen your ability to transfer thought into a realized emotion in your body. Though you can contemplate the thought, it is a no-thing to you. That is when joy ceases, for how can you be joyous over a thought unless you can become it through the feeling of it?

When you are unable to feel, you are unable to register knowingness on this plane. That is the harm you do to your brain when you partake of what you term your weed or drugs that cause illusions to occur. Each time you partake of these things, they remove oxygen from your brain. It is the dying of your brain that causes what you term the high that you feel. That is why it occurs. Each time you do this, you restrict your ability to know. And there will come a time when you cannot weep or laugh, for there is no longer anything strong enough to create emotion within your being.

To experience all-knowingness — where you can weep over the opening of a flower or wait for the sun to come up and know every bit of its splendor — is to have the ability to know, to compute thought into feeling. That is called ecstasy. That is a good high, as you term it.

That which has loved you since before time began — who has been with you in every life you have ever lived, who is the only entity that will be with you in the death of your body or the ascension of it — is you. You are the only one who loves you steadfastly enough to go through all the things you have gone through. When you embrace and love yourself and allow that love to be your standard, you will transcend the social consciousness of man into the all-consciousness of God, for what you are goes beyond beauty. It goes beyond perfection. It goes beyond the containment of laws and dogma and social standards. It goes into destiny, into the fulfillment of self, which is the fulfillment of God. That is the only thing that is important in the eyes of the Isness of life.

You are all that you think you are and all that you allow yourself to know. Know that the Father, that is all things, is that which you are, and through that knowingness will you know and become all that is.

Know that there is no end to anything and there is no absoluteness to anything. Everything is in the moment and there is always more to come. To unlimit your thinking is simply to know that there is greater truth, and there is even greater truth than that. Know that, and it will occur to you according to your state of receivership.

Never allow yourself to be enslaved or intimidated. There is always a way, and a better way. Know that, and allow the thoughts to come to you that will light your path to joy.

Face your limitations. Embrace them. Master them. Do away with all the things in your life that keep you from knowing the totality of God. Relinquish guilt and judgment so you can allow knowingness, answers, and joy to come forth.

Face your fears and allow yourself to unmask their illusion. Know that you are forever and that there is nothing in the unknown that can ever keep you from happiness and joy. Do away with the fear that inhibits you from knowing something greater than what you are experiencing on this plane. Why, you even think those who come here from afar are scary. Your brothers in great aeroships have incredible beauty. Do away with fear so that you have the ability to befriend another time, another space, another entity from another dimension.

In striving to become greater, if you look upon this plane to find a greatness to become, all you will ever become is what is on this plane. To go beyond the limited thinking of man is to contemplate that perhaps there is something as yet unseen that is more vast in its understanding.

Be open to truth, regardless of its source, and let your feelings be your guide. The wise man, even be he blind, knows within his soul what feels right. Truth is even in the blade of grass that you tread upon. It is in the laughter of a child. It is in the eyes of a beggar. It is in all places and all things, in all peoples and all moments. He who does not know this does not know God, for God is everything that is. And not one blade of grass, not one whisper of a moment can separate itself from the Source of all that is. Learn to be wise. Listen to truth, whatever form it comes in, and know that you are worthy of receiving it.

He who knows that the kingdom of heaven lies within him is a wise entity. With your capacity to think any thought and feel it within your soul, you possess within you the keys to the kingdom of heaven, the treasure of emotion. Learn to feel. To know God completely is to feel every thought completely until every thought that God is, is felt within the core of your being, the soul of your being.

Don't overwhelm yourself by wanting the totality of your brain to open all at once. Have it open up thought by thought, experience by experience, so that each thought will solidify in you.

Above all, allow yourself to be for, in being, you are everything. When you are simply the Isness of yourself, the I-Am principle, then you are in alignment with the whole of life. Then you have transformed the alienation of yourself as man into oneness with God.

***

CHAPTER 20

The Virtue Of Experience

You are loved even beyond your understanding of love, for you have never been seen as anything other than a God struggling to understand who and what it is.

In your adventures into the exploration of thought, you have chosen to express through the cellular form called humanity so that you could learn all there is to learn of the human experience, of God living in the limited form called matter. This experience is necessary for the complete understanding of God, for how can you understand unlimitedness until you experience and understand limitedness? How can you understand the totality of yourself, God that you are, until you experience and embrace the totality of what God is, from the wild expanse of pure thought, all the way to the restrictiveness of matter? How can you understand joy, freedom, and foreverness until you experience sorrow, limitation, and the illusion of death?

Though you play out your games and illusions with great and terrible seriousness, all they are really there for is to teach you, to expand you, to enlighten you, to help you understand you. This life is simply a platform upon which your games can be played and your illusions experienced for the greatest prize of life called wisdom.

What is wisdom? 'Tis a most wondrous treasure that belongs wholly to the God within man, a treasure which is collected within the soul of man. Wisdom is the collection of emotions gained from all of your adventures into the realms of thought called God, and it is the only thing you take with you when you leave this place. Do you think you take your wondrous linens, or your great mansions, or your auto machines that go very fast? What do you think you take with you? You take what you are, all the emotions gained from your journey into the principle called life. Emotion is what life is all about.

All that mankind has learned through the tyranny and restrictiveness of religious and governmental rule — through the separation and debasement of the races, through the separation of men from women and brother from brother — has been realized through the demeaning of God in what is perhaps the lowest ebb ever. Yet you never would have known what it felt like to overtake another in battle, to deny another's freedom, to degrade women and make them less than men, unless you had experienced all of those things. You never would have emotionally known those things unless you had first become the creator who dreamed them into a reality and then purposefully lived the dream. Yet in living it life after life and moment to moment, it has become such a steadfast reality that most have become neurotic, insecure, and utterly lost in the dream.

Where is this God, you ask, that would allow mankind to be so beastly unto itself? And where is God's love, after all, if he has permitted these atrocities to occur? Well, God has been there all along, for he has been all of your illusions and all of your games. And God certainly has loved you all along, for he has allowed you to experience your dreams according to your own designs. You simply have forgotten that you created the dream in the first place and that you have the option to change it at any moment you choose.

You weave your illusions into tales of great woe and sadness. You are destructive to your bodies. You do away with your minds. You worship idols. You are critical of others. You are judgmental, hateful, possessive, fearful, and indeed arrogant. And yet for what purpose? To understand what it is to be all of those things. What is the end result? Never to die but to live forever, to understand and embrace what is called the kingdom of heaven, to look upon the face of God and realize it is your own.

All of you eminent entities — trapped by your own insecurities, your own pettiness of thought — you are far greater than the games you have played which have hidden, deep beneath your illusions, the sublime beauty that you are. If you only knew how powerful and splendid you are, you wouldn't curse or judge or alter yourselves in the ways that you do.

Unto you come I — and I am all that you have been and all you shall become — to help rekindle in you the knowingness that you already possess so you never again lose yourselves and wallow in guilt and fear and self-denial. You are indeed far greater than that.

Why do I love you so deeply? For what you are, I am also. All that you are, in the spectrum of your being, be I, for I am the spectrum from which you contemplate and create your illusions. The I Am that I am is love that transcends the common expression here, for it has no conditions or musts. I love you simply for who you are, for who you are — however you express — is the Father that I love greatly.

Now I desire to speak to you about what you perceive to be your wrongs and failings.

Man's creation of right and wrong, perfect and imperfect, has also created the entrapments called guilt and remorse, which have made it ever so difficult to progress in life. But I tell you, entities, whatever you have done — through the virtue of your many lives upon this plane — has never been bad and it has never been good. It has been simply an experience of life that has helped to make you who you are now. And that is indeed a most precious and wondrous thing, for you are in this Now the greatest you have ever been since you began this remarkable journey, because your wisdom is greater than it has ever been.

All you have ever done, I have done the same. And for all your errors, I have made as many. And all the things you judge in yourself as being without strength and virtue, I have had also. But I never would have known the strength of my being until I knew the weakness of my being. I never would have loved life until I saw it ebbing from me. And I never would have been able to embrace all of you until I despised the cruelty of man.

Whatever you have done— however vile or wretched it has been — you have done simply for the purpose of creating learning for yourself. And through that learning you have hurt, you have pained, you have sorrowed, you have degraded yourself, and yet you have arisen from it because here you are now ready to know and embrace the beauty that you are.

For those of you who feel that you have failed or done something wrong, I desire that you contemplate this. From the moment of your birth, you and your beloved brothers set about on a grand adventure into the emotional understanding of all thought, thought by thought by thought. Your soul was created to store the emotion of each thought — each dimension of God — that you accept through the God or Spirit of your being. Each thought you have accepted and felt within your soul. But which you have yet to completely understand, your soul will press you to experience. Why? To gain the complete emotional understanding of all aspects of that thought seen only through the virtue of experience, which is the virtue called life.

You have been driven throughout eternity to evolve and expand life into creativity and to experience every manifestation of that creativity from thought into light, into matter, into form, and back again into thought; from love and joy to envy, hate, and sorrow, and back again to joy. Your soul has driven you from experience to experience, adventure to adventure, so it can fulfill itself in the complete understanding of every form of thought — every attitude, every emotion — so that you may know and understand the totality of thought, which is the totality of God, which is the totality of self.

Your soul hungers for what it has never experienced. When your soul hungers for an experience, it means that it needs emotional data from that experience. So your soul will create a feeling — called want — that captivates your entire being and propels you into an adventure, an experience. Then when the experience is finished and the emotions from it have subsided, the experience gained you a grander treasure than all the gold upon your plane. It advanced you into wisdom, which is indicative of your soul saying you never have to experience that again, for you have gained all the understanding from it. Then your soul will take on another hunger, and you will be propelled to do other things because you need to, you want to, because the fire within you presses you to experience all life.

Now do you think you ever set about to experience something, knowing that it was wrong for you or that you would fail? No. You have always embarked upon every adventure with great curiosity, interest, and delight. Even though at the outset the outcome was a little unknown, you undertook it simply because you hadn't done it before. The experience was new and exciting and you wanted to learn from it. And though pain may have been experienced in the adventure, it helped you to understand the emotion called pain, which added to your understanding of life. So that experience was purposeful in your life. Then you embarked upon the next adventure that your soul urged you to experience for yet another adventure into emotion and understanding. And that brought you a happiness and fulfillment within your soul.

Everything you do, the very moment you are doing it, you know within your soul that the experience is right for you. It is only after you have experienced the adventure and the feelings derived from it have settled into wisdom that you ascertain that perhaps you could have done it better or differently. But you never would have known there was a betterment until first you had embarked on the experience and procured from it the jewel of wisdom. Should anyone be judged for that? No, for that is called innocence and it is also called education.

Failure is a reality only for those who believe it is. But no one truly fails at life — ever. In spite of each thing you have done — each wretched, despicable, secretive thing, which really is not — you are still alive, a miraculous occurrence. To fail would mean to stop. Yet nothing can ever stop, for life is ongoing; it advances every moment. So you can never stand still or go backward in life, for each moment of life's ongoing expansion always brings on greater and greater understanding.

You have never failed; you have always learned. How do

you know what happiness is until you have been unhappy? How do you know what your goal is until you have approached it and found it to be a different color than you had envisioned it?

You have never made a mistake — ever. You have never done anything wrong. What is there to feel guilty for? All of your wrongs, your failings, your errors, are what are called appropriately steps to God, step by step. And to know all that you now know could only have been achieved by taking the steps.

Never feel guilty about learning. Never feel guilty about wisdom. That is called enlightenment. You must understand that you have done what you needed to do; it was all necessary. And you made all the right choices, all of them. You are going to live tomorrow and indeed the blessed day thereafter, and on and on and on. And what you shall discover in those days is that you know more than you knew this day. Yet this day is not a mistake. It will lead you into forever.

You have the option to create your dream however you choose. But however you create it, for your own purposeful understanding, you add to the whole of consciousness everywhere. You never take away from it; you can never take away from it. Every adventure you happily undertake adds to the fervor and intensity of life. Every thought you embrace, every illusion you experience, every discovery you make, every vile and wretched thing you do, broadens your understanding, which in turn feeds and broadens the consciousness of all mankind and expands the mind of God.

If you think you have failed in life or done anything wrong, you lessen your ability to perceive your own inner and outer greatness and your importance to the whole of life. Never desire to remove any of your past — not any of it — because the friction from all your sublime and wretched experiences has produced within your soul the great and beauteous pearls of wisdom. That means you never again have to dream those dreams, create those games, or experience those experiences, for you have experienced them and know what they feel like and have the record of them in your soul — called feelings — the truest treasure of life.

I am here to tell you that you are loved even beyond your

understanding of love, for you have never been seen as anything other than a God struggling to understand itself. And from every experience in all of your lives, you have gained knowledge, wisdom. You have given to the world. You have added to the virtue of unfolding life.

Your life has been a wonderful spectacle of the fire that lives within you. It should be reviewed in reverence, holiness, divineness, for no matter what you do, you are always God. No matter what mask you wear, you are God. No matter what relationship you are experiencing, you are still God.

You are worthy of this life's adventures, every single one of them. And far greater, you are worthy of the splendid adventures that yet await. But you shan't ever become the I Am or enter the doors of eternity until you realize that all you have done, you have done simply to gain the understanding of the God that you are, which is demonstrated here and now through the virtue of all your experiences upon the platform called life.

So you who carry your baggage of burdens heavily upon your back, if it makes you happy to do so, so be it. But if you have learned all there is to learn from them and you are tired of them, get rid of them. How? By loving them, embracing them, and allowing them to be in your being. Once you have done that, they shan't ever hold you again. And from there, the wonderment of life can be seen through clear eyes, love can be felt without judgment, and the joy of being can become the power of unlimited knowingness.

Embrace your life. Know that you are divine and that the strength of your being is there because of all you have done. Cease the guilt. Cease the mockery of sadness in self. Cease burdening yourself. Cease placing the blame on everyone else. Take hold of it. It belongs to you.

Now what happens when you have embraced all that you have judged, loved all you have despised, lived all of your illusions, pursued all of your dreams? You can look at others who are experiencing those things for their learning, and you can understand and have compassion for them. Then you can love them as the Father loves you, and you can allow them the virtue of their own life experiences. Then you become what you call a saint.

How do you think you become saintly? Certainly not by abstaining from life, by hiding yourself in a cave or a temple and burning incense, or sitting atop a tall mountain and contemplating God-knows-what. You become a saint only by living life — which the Father is — and experiencing it to the ultimate so that the virtue of wisdom culminates into an entity who can embrace the whole of mankind and love it.

The only way to know and become God is to live and embrace life completely, to experience all situations, feel all emotions, do every sublime and wretched deed, so that your soul has the wisdom of all life within it.

You never know what the king suffers until you are a king. And the king never knows the humbleness of his servant until he becomes a servant. And the pious woman knows not the hardships of the concubine until she is one. And the concubine knows not the judgment of the pious woman until she is one. Thus the path to a virtuous life is all-encompassing. It includes every character, every illusionary situation created within the consciousness of man. That is why the wisest, most noble entities have lived every situation created by the adventures of mankind. They have been the harlot and the priest, the guru and the farmer, the murderer and the murdered, the conqueror and the conquered, the child and the parent.

You see, you only condemn in others what you cannot accept within yourself. If you have lived all situations and found peace with them, then it is easy to understand everyone and allow them to be, without judgment, because you have been them and you know that if you judge them, you are judging yourself. Then you have gained the virtue of true compassion, and the depths of love shall exist within your soul. Then you are indeed a Christ, for you understand, love, and forgive your beloved brothers in their limitations.

To love the Father in his totality, to be his totality, is to love all that he is. And all that he is, is your beloved brothers all around you. No matter what they look like, they are God in their reality as you are God in yours. And when you have lived all of their glory, all of their struggles, all of their sorrow and joy, then you can embrace God seen in all people. Then you can love them. That does not mean you must go out and teach them or succor unto them. Simply leave them alone and allow them to evolve according to their own needs and designs. There are those whose destiny is to be a warlord or a priest or a caller in the marketplace, because that is what they need and want to do. Who are you to take that from them?

Everyone in this world — whether he is starving or crippled or a farmer or a king — has chosen his experience for the purpose of gaining from it. Only when he has learned from it and is filled with it will he go onto yet another experience, which will bring forth yet greater understanding of his innermost self.

When you become a master, you can walk into the murk and mire of limited consciousness and maintain your totality because you understand the teeming masses and why they are the way they are, because once you were that way. You will allow them the freedom to be limited — which is true love— because you know that that is the only way they can learn to have unlimited understanding and to love one another, which of course is to love themselves wholly. And when see you another face in the crowd — regardless of its color or cleanliness or appearance — you will look at the entity and see God in them because if you look closely enough, you will find God in everyone. Then you love as the Father loves. Then you see what he sees, not only in you but in everyone else. When you can look at everyone and see the beauty that they are, you are on your way to ascending from this plane into a grander space where there are many mansions. But the doors are closed to one who cannot wholly embrace himself and the God that lives in all life around him.

When you put people back where they belong, in their godhead, and know that no matter what they are doing, they are living for the God within them — just as you are living for the God within you — then you can learn to love all people. Whatever their expression is, you can now for the first time in your existence truly love them, for your love is not governed or restrained by judgments. And that indeed is how a Christ — man who lives as God — is within his being.

What is your path in life? To always follow your feelings, to listen to the feelings within your soul and embark upon the adventures that your soul urges you to experience. Your soul, if you listen to it, will tell you what you need to experience. If you are feeling bored or have no desire to do something, it means you have already experienced it and have collected the wisdom from that adventure. But if you want to do something, that urging within your soul means you must have the experience, the virtue of it. If you abstain from it, you are only postponing the experience until another moment or another existence.

Live the truth of what you feel inside and love who is feeling it. Understand that the feeling must be expressed and fulfilled. If you want to do any one thing, regardless of what it is, it would not be wise to go against that feeling, for there is an experience awaiting you and a grand adventure that will make your life sweeter. If you listen to your feelings, you will always be doing the right thing for the evolution of your beauteous self into profound wisdom. It is when you go against your feelings that you have sickness of the body, neurosis, and despair.

Follow your heart, your dreams, your desires. Do what your soul calls you to do, whatever it is, and allow it to be finished. Then you will go on to another adventure. You will never be judged unless you accept the judgment of those around you. And if you accept their judgment, it is only your will to do so for the experience.

There will come a time, whether in this life or in those that follow, when you have reached the point where you have no desire to do this or that but only to be. You no longer desire to curse or judge the harlot, the thief, the murderer, or the warring country for its deeds. You will have been all of those things and you will know how it feels to be the way they are. You are so complete in the experiences of this plane that no longer is there anything that you will be drawn back here to experience. Then you are off to new adventures on greater planes of being.

When you contemplate what I have just told you, you

will perceive and understand a value in yourself that is the purposeful demonstration of the powerful God, the fire, the life that you are. You will also understand that whichever way you desire to direct yourself in life, that is the path for your enlightenment and, from every adventure along the way, you will gain a greater perception of the mystery of yourself. You will come to love what you are and cherish it, burnish it, to where the light of your being can compete with the great Ra in your heavens, and the peace of your being can compete with midnight, when all is quiet on the land. You will never deny yourself ever again. You will never alter what you are. You will never judge what you are. You will allow what you are to be.

When you love what you are, then you can say with grace, dignity, and humble strength, "The Father do I love greatly, for the Father and I are one. And I love what I am greatly, for the I Am that I am is the essence of all that is." Then you are in harmony with the flow of life. You are a master who walks the plane. You are the arisen Christ, the awakened Christ. You are a light to the world. But you cannot become that until you love and embrace everything you have done and realize that it was all for the purposeful good of your life, because it has made you the magnificent entity that you are this day.

I have given you a grand teaching in a grand sort of way, for it gets you off the hook from karma, sin, judgment, and retribution, for the Father is love. And the Father is without judgment. The Father is without good or bad. It is without positive and negative. The Father is simply the Isness that is. And that Isness encompasses all people, all deeds, all thoughts, all emotions, all things. If the Father could ever judge you, he certainly would be judging himself, for you and he are one and the same.

So the love of God called life has always been given to you. Regardless of all your wretched experiences, the sun has still come up and danced across the heavens. The seasons have still come and gone. The wildfowl still fly to a northern sky. And the nighthawk still squawks as you close the shutters of your room. You see, it is in the ongoingness of those things where, if you look, you will realize the forgiveness and foreverness that life has always bestowed upon you.

Go from this audience with a light and loving heart, for your burdens, they have been taken from you. Your redemption, it is certain. Know that God loves you and always has. Know that you are not evil, nor are you good. Know that you are neither perfect nor imperfect, that you simply are. Expect the Father to be in your life, for he has always been there. And whenever you contemplate love, think of me, and from nowhere will come the wind.

***

CHAPTER 21

One Fine Morn

*I shall be with you throughout all the days of your life, as
your precious soul blooms into a magnificent flower of
wisdom, compassion, and the love to embrace all life.*

These moments we have shared together have been sweet.
To come into your life and touch perhaps even the edge of it is a
grand pleasure, I assure you. All I have shared with you, I have
done for myself, for each of you are what I am, the Father that I
love fervently and always will. Whatever I do to add to the
evolvement of your precious beings glorifies and magnifies the
Father that is the kingdom I Am.

I have come as a brother to mankind, of which I was once
a fervent part. I lived here as man and experienced all that you
have experienced. I lived your despair and wept your sorrow. I
dreamed your dreams and knew your joy. Though I have been to
all levels, the most profound of all my experiences was when I
was here in the midst of you as man, God/man, experiencing the
perils, the desperation, and the fleeting moments of glory that all
of you have known. I have chosen to come back here because I
understand you. And to understand you is to love you.

I have come not to save you, for there is really nothing to
save you from. I have come simply to remind you of the wonderful
heritage you forgot long ago and to tell you of a glorious future
you are all soon to see. I have come to help you realize that you
have greater options for your life's expression and to help bring
forth the knowledge that allows you to exercise those options, if

it is your will to do so. All I have asked of you is to apply in your life — in your own time and in your own way — whatever understandings are fruitful for you in your own evolution into a more harmonious and joyful life.

My path in my life upon this plane was to become the Unknown God — which I was to discover was myself — and to go beyond the dimensions to frolic in the adventures of forever. And so I did, and still do. I have returned to tell you that those adventures are awaiting you also, when you have embraced all of this life as I did.

Go and live the understandings I have given you. Let them be within your being. When you do, you will soon realize that you have been given a greater treasure than you could ever have asked for or conceived of.

Take what you have learned, what you have heard, what you have read, and apply it with simplicity. The simpler you are, the more powerful you become. And if you want something, ask for it. No one on this plane is empowered to give it to you. Ask from the Lord God of your being that the Father give it to you and know that he has, regardless of what it is. And where do you go to ask? To the temple within. Simply ask within the silence of your own thoughts. It is always heard.

I know who you are. And I know what you do and what you dream. When you think no one sees you, you must understand that you are like the stars in the heavens at midnight. You are there for all to see. All things know who you are and what you do, particularly those of us in the unseen.

Who you are really matters only to you. When all is said and done, you have only you to depend upon and that precious light within you called God Almighty. Be even with yourself. Be individual with yourself. And love what you are so that your light and how you are seen, like the stars at midnight, becomes very bright and very beautiful.

I was called Ramtha the Enlightened One by my people, and so I have kept that name even unto this hour. An enlightened one? I was a solitary entity who sat on a plateau while everyone else busied themselves with all of the things they do in their days.

Yet in that wilderness, alienated from everyday life, I found the Unknown God.

The world is not in the marketplace, my beloved brothers. It teems there with life indeed. But the greater life is to be found outside of the marketplace at the base of a magnificent tree, or on top of a snowy mountain where the wind is crisp and cold and clean, or in the openness of the desert, or upon the endlessness of the sea. There is so much more to this your plane than most of you have allowed yourselves to see. You have yet to really live and investigate it. You have only been in the oppressive consciousness of your society, with its judgments and petty ideals and its mad race against the illusion of time.

You will not truly know life until you have become solitary in such places, at peace with the midnight sky and the moon that waxes and wanes until the brilliance of dawn. And through all the knowledge and dreams that come to you, behold, you too will become the enlightened one, for priorities change there. The consciousness of the wilderness accepts you, beloved brothers. It accepts you and it expects you to be timeless, like it is. In such circumstances do you grow to become this God and to become steadfast in all the days of your life.

The Unknown God is silence — great silence — and yet it speaks to you if you allow it to do so. Reach out and be a part of this continent. Go to all of its places. Be a part of them. Put down your silks and jewels and take your shoes off. Be cluttered with unfashionable simpleness and go and experience God in this your heaven that you have created. I beseech you to do this. You will not truly have lived — nor will you come to understand this God that you are — until you have been to these places and been a part of their ongoing, forever consciousness.

I desire from the totality of my being, from the Father that burns within me, that you know how valuable you are and the extent to which you are loved and needed. Whenever you think you have none who cares whether you live or die, know that I do. And whenever the preciousness of your being begins to falter and you feel you need a companion, call upon me, for I shall be there.

I shall be with all of you throughout all the days of your lives on this plane as your precious souls — pregnant with love and hope and joy — bloom into magnificent flowers of wisdom, compassion, and the love to embrace all life, seen and unseen. In the emotional storm of that blooming, there will be moments when you will wish you had never heard the name Ramtha, but far, far greater indeed will be the moments when God is seen, realized, and known within you.

Now I have told you in every conceivable way — and over and over and over again — of the grandest truth you will ever know: You are God. And you are beginning to realize perhaps that that is indeed a truth. To know that steadfastly, beloved masters, can come only through the moment-to-moment unfoldment of your life.

But I desire for you to know this: One fine morn, in the moments before dawn, as you lie alone in your bed and the quiet is so quiet it can be heard, you will awaken from a dream that is not a dream. You will open your eyes to the dark of your room, arise from your pallet, and walk to a window that provides the only light to be seen.

You will peer through the window, its sill cluttered with droplets of dew, into the dark gray of a morning to gaze upon the heavens that hold the promise of a grand and brilliant light. And as you look upon the beauty of all the brilliant, little jewels sparkling against the dark, velvet backdrop of forever, you see that the moon has waxed and waned and now sits silently upon the horizon, awaiting a greater light.

Alone, quivering with a feeling beyond any words, you sit there gazing into the quiet of awakening life. Soon you hear a rustling in the brush from a bird who, like you, has arisen from its bed to prepare itself to salute the morn. As you listen to his sweet and mellow song of hope and joy, you turn your vision to the East to look upon the distant horizon. And there you see the lonely, purpled mountains, like sentinels to life, looming tall and quiet and strong, silhouetted by a pale light, the color of rose. And the clouds that have made a silent journey onto the horizon are outlined in the gold of a promising dawn.

At one with all this splendor in its simplicity of being, you hear no thing except the beating of your heart as it pounds in anticipation of a grand event soon to be seen in a blaze of glory upon the horizon. As the curtain of night slowly fades into the light of morn, you see the stars grow fainter and fainter, and the moon in her magic surrenders her beauty to the unfolding dawn.

As you are caught up in the beauty and the rapture of the moment, there comes this realization. Without the ongoingness of that morn, all of your fears, your worries, your dreams, and your illusions would be no-things. At that moment there appears, rising from behind the gilded mountains, the splendor of a fiery jewel, its golden rods piercing the misty valley like brilliant beams of hope. As the great Ra rises higher and higher, the sky becomes afire with colors of blue and lavender and rose, orange and deep red. And the bird sings louder and begins its flight as all of the world awakens to the promise and wonderful breath of morn.

As you gaze at this spectacular view that has seen all moments of time, and the emotion of its wonderment seizes your entire being, you will soar with the realization that you are indeed the life of Ra. You are the strong and quiet sentinels to life towering on the distant horizon. You are indeed the colors of the awakening dawn, the movement of the branches in the brush, the drops of dew upon the windowsill, and the morning bird's sweet and mellow song of joy.

And the next dawn that you see will be seen as Behold God That I Am. And you will be caught up in the majesty and the beauty of all that is, for you are now one with the light and the power and the ongoingness of this force that speaks no word.

To learn of a truth is one thing; to become it is quite another. But when you least expect it, you will arise to gaze at such a splendor in the sky. And the knowingness of this truth, through the peace of being, will become a reality one fine morn. Then all of the words, the confusion, the anger, the rejection of self, the complexities of understanding God, the searching, the books, and the teachers, will have ended in quiet, through a profound realization that has no words.

Your morning is coming, as came mine.

Other Ramtha Titles

The following is a list of additional books on Ramtha that can be purchased through Ramtha's School of Enlightenment and other fine bookstores. Also available is a whole library of recordings and videos of Ramtha's teachings. All products are available through mail order at:

Ramtha's School of Enlightenment
P.O. Box 519
Yelm, Washington 98597 USA
800.347-0439 or 360.458.4771
www.ramtha.com
mailorder@ramtha.com

RAMTHA

#1401.1 Spanish	$17.00
#1401.2 French	$21.95
#1401.3 German	$16.50
#1401.4 Norwegian	$18.95
#1401.5 Italian	$20.00
#1401.8 Japanese	$19.95

RAMTHA: AN INTRODUCTION *Edited by Steven L. Weinberg, Ph.D. (228 pages).* An engaging collection of teachings that will appeal equally to those familiar or unfamiliar with Ramtha. More than an introduction; a true treasure of personal mastery.

#1404 - Softcover	$ 9.95
#1404G German	$16.00
#1404I Italian	$15.00
#1404S Spanish	$14.00

I AM RAMTHA *Edited by Richard Cohn, Cindy Black, and Greg Simmons (127 pages).* This book is a beautifully photographed book that accompanies thirteen of Ramtha's most universal teachings. Wonderful teachings on the subject of feelings, being at one with nature, unconditional love, and the prize that is called life.

#1201 - Hardcover	$9.95

THE ANCIENT SCHOOLS OF WISDOM *Compiled by Diane Munoz-Smith (172 pages).* This is an introduction to the formation of Ramtha's School of Enlightenment. Ramtha tells how the ancient schools operated in times past and why their instruction was so precise to awaken the forgotten God within.

#7100 - Softcover	$19.95
#7100G German	$21.00
#7100I Italian	$15.00
#7100S Spanish	$17.00

A BEGINNER'S GUIDE TO CREATING REALITY *Ramtha (138 pages).*This book consists of the original teachings that are given to students who come to Ramtha's School of Enlightenment for their first weekend training.

#7223 - Hardcover	$14.95
#7223G German	$20.00
#7223I Italian	$11.00
#7223S Spanish	$15.00

THE PLANE OF BLISS *Ramtha (154 pages).* What happens between incarnations? This book describes topics that are essentially the barest mystery of human wondering and human contemplation.

#7227 - Softcover	$10.95
#7227S Spanish	$16.00

THE CHILDREN'S VIEW OF DESTINY AND PURPOSE *Ramtha (50 pages).* This children's book, illustrated by the children who attended this teaching, is a simple and yet profound understanding of life's destiny and life's purpose.

#1460 - Hardcover	$14.95

STATE OF MIND: MY STORY *JZ Knight (445 pages).* The intimate account of JZ's life in her own words. Her story, which includes her humorous and poignant introduction to Ramtha, is a story of the triumph of the human Spirit.

#1501 - Hardcover	$9.95
#1501.1 - Cassette (120 minutes)	$9.95

TO LIFE *Compiled by Diane Munoz-Smith.* At the beginning of each audience, Ramtha elegantly and thought-provokingly salutes the God within with a toast. This book is a selection of the toasts from Ramtha's audiences from May 1988 - May 1996.
#7101 - Softcover $15.95

LAST WALTZ OF THE TYRANTS *Edited by Judy Pope Koteen (153 pages).* This book is a synthesis of Ramtha's teachings on the challenges we face by those who control the world economy and from the coming radical changes in nature.
#1202 - Softcover $13.95
#1202I Italian $12.00
#1202S Spanish $12.00
#1202F French $20.00
#1202G German $13.00

UFO'S AND THE NATURE OF REALITY *Edited by Judy Pope Koteen (221 pages).* This book tells the story of alien intervention in our history, in our present time, and in our future. It exposes the limitations of subjective mind and encourages the reader to move into interdimensional mind.
#1611 - Softcover $11.00
#1611G German $19.95
#1611I Italian $15.00
#1611S Spanish $14.00

SPINNER OF TALES *Compiled by Deborah Kerins (228 pages).* Ramtha has captivated audiences throughout the years with his telling of tales. Now they have been put together in book form to be preserved and delight readers of all ages.
#1300 - Softcover $10.00

FINANCIAL FREEDOM *Edited by Judy Pope Zion (126 pages)* "If you think there is a demarcation between gold and God, you are not only a hypocrite, you are cutting your own throat."
#1205 - Softcover $13.95
#1205G German $15.00
#1205S Spanish $12.00

SOULMATES, THE INTENSIVE *Ramtha (128 pages)*. Based on a 3-day workshop, Ramtha spells out the mystery of the science of soulmates and its importance in knowing and loving self.

#1403 - Softcover	$10.00
#1403G German	$13.50
#1403I Italian	$15.00
#1403F French	$13.50

CHANGE: THE DAYS TO COME *Ramtha (149 pages)*. This book is based on the 1986 teachings that challenged the audience to become self-sufficient in order to survive the dramatic changes in nature and society that will occur throughout the world.

#1402 - Softcover	$10.00
#1402G German	$14.50
#1402F French	$14.95

Videos and Foreign Language Products

We have a growing selection of Ramtha books, audio cassettes, and videos in German, Italian, Spanish, French, and Japanese.

CREATING PERSONAL REALITY *(5-volume video set)*. This is a 9-1/2 hour instructional teaching given to all beginning students their first weekend at Ramtha's School of Enlightenment.

#1.42	$89.95
German, Italian, Spanish, French	$120
Japanese	$165

INTIMATE CONVERSATIONS *(27 minutes-NTSC/PAL)*. Two distinct beings - JZ Knight and Ramtha - one ancient, one modern, sharing provocative insights about God, about love, and about life.

#1.40	$19.95
German, Italian, Spanish, French	$24.95
Japanese	$40.00

A LOOK WITHIN *(32 minutes-NTSC/PAL)*. This is the first video that highlights the disciplines done at the school. Included are interviews with students, scholars, and JZ Knight.

#1.46	$19.95
German, Italian, Spanish, French	$24.95
Japanese	$40.00

TWO PATHS *(7 hours - 3 videos)*. This is a teaching on the ministry of Jeshua ben Joseph, Jesus the Christ. It describes the "two paths" available to every individual: the emotional body of humanity and its agreement in mind control, and the second path, our natural path, which is God.

#1.60	$49.95

THE MAGICAL BRAIN *(106 minutes-NTSC/PAL)*. Ramtha shares his insights of the brain and how to harness its enormous power for manifestation.

#1.12	$30.00